SHELLS

A comprehensive guide to the treasures of the beach

Grange
BOOKS

A QUANTUM BOOK

Published by Grange Books
an imprint of Grange Books Ltd.
35, Riverside
Sir Thomas Longley Road
Medway City Estate, Rochester
Kent ME2 4DP
www.grangebooks.co.uk

Copyright © 2004 Quantum Publishing Ltd.

This edition printed 2008

ISBN: 978-1-84804-007-6

QUMSHELL

Contents

Introduction

Seashells are exquisite wonders of nature which have demanded a response from mankind, and indeed have been inextricably linked with the human story since the dawn of civilization. The appreciation, study, enjoyment and collecting of seashells is probably as widespread now as at any time in history. Appreciation, because few have failed to be intrigued and amazed at their diversity and complexity of colour, shape and form; shells have stimulated the artistic, promoted ideas in design and architecture, inspired musicians and poets and have led to the publication of some of the most beautiful books ever produced for natural historians.

Scientifically known as marine molluscs, seashells are the hard outer covering of highly adaptable snails that inhabit the world's oceans in a wide range of environments and at varying depths. These shells can be found washed ashore, emptied of the soft bodies that once inhabited them, in rock pools, beneath mud and sand at low tide, and beneath the seas in shallow waters and down to dark abyssal depths. As objects of scientific study, shells have much to offer. They are of interest to medical research, in general education and in relation to environmental and ecological issues. Most importantly, they are also an important food source and are linked to the relatively new science known as mariculture.

The 'golden age' of shell collecting was during the 200 years of discovery and exploration that drew to a close at the turn of this century, but conchology – as the study and collecting of shells is correctly termed – has entered a new era. Thanks to modern fishing methods, rare shells that were once known only from a handful of old and faded specimens in museum vaults are now available to all. Modern colour photography captures the intricate beauty of shells in all their wonder and there are many excellent books on the subject.

Conchologists and amateur collectors have an infectious enthusiasm, and along with the increasing awareness of the need for environmental protection is a growing need to discover more about the natural world. I believe that conchology will continue to enhance mankind in both work and leisure for generations to come.

The influence of shells on art and architecture

Shells are, and always have been, a great source of inspiration for artists. Of all shells, the scallop has perhaps been most frequently used – ornamenting roman lead coffins, decorating niches and porticoes, carved above church doorways, chosen by

Fossil shells

When you consider the wealth and complexity of natural forms, and especially of molluscan design, it is hard to believe that they all 'just happened.' Science argues that molluscs derive from a unifying original life form, but the evolution of molluscs cannot easily be traced or explained. Some genera clearly developed and changed under environmental influences, while others ceased to exist, but there is no scientifically proven common ancestor of all the mollusc species known today. Several present day species, such as chambered nautilus and species of slit-shells, have unsevered links with the very earliest geological times. These incredible shells have withstood the passage of time without noticeable change, while other far less sophisticated and adaptable species have disappeared and are known only from fossils.

Some species, such as the tusk shells, have changed little in shape since they first appeared, while others have evolved considerably. There is a vast range of molluscs, often with bizarre shapes, which can only be found in fossil form. These include Caprine, Spinigera and early long-spined forms of the family Aporrhaidae, all of which provide a fascinating subject for study.

Gastropods, bivalves, scaphopods and cephalopods are all well represented in fossil records, but species of the order polyplacophora, although first appearing in the late Cambrian period, are scarce and rare. Monoplacophora, another very ancient group, also date back to early Cambrian.

With the onset of the Mesozoic era, a great increase in family and generic increase took place – especially among shells of the Volutidae, Muricidae and Cerithiidae families. During the Tertiary era, especially the Eocene period, the gastropods were the most numerous of all molluscs and many species have changed little from that time to the present day. Significant numbers of bivalves did not appear until the late Devonian and early Carboniferous periods, when swampy conditions appear to have suited them.

Botticelli as a vehicle for Venus rising from the waves and in modern times picked as the logo for the Shell Oil Company.

Leonardo da Vinci made drawings of spiral shells and one of these is thought to have provided the inspiration for the famous spiral staircase at the Château de Blois in France.

Nautilus shells were used for goblets and chalices in the 16th and 17th centuries, while in the 19th century sailors returning from a long voyage would make shell collages as Valentines for their sweethearts.

above: The Birth of Venus by Botticelli.

The nomenclature and classification of molluscs

Most living things are referred to by their common or colloquial names. Shells, for example, are often just called 'whelks,' 'cockles' or 'conch' and so on. However, this can be very misleading and confusing when you realize that these names can vary greatly from place to place and country to country. All natural creatures and plants, including shells, have therefore been given a two-part Latin name which has been universally adopted.

The name of a particular species of seashell is structured as follows. Let us take, for example, a popular and large species, commonly known as the triton's trumpet, but correctly named thus: Charonia tritonis. Linné 1758.

The first of the two Latin names refers to the genus, the group to which this species and its close relatives belong and is correctly started with a capital letter. The second name, not capitalized, is the species or specific name. Generic names cannot be used for more than one group of animals and the specific name cannot be used for any other species in that particular genus.

For every species so described there is an authority, known as the author – the biologist, scientist or even layman who first published a valid description of this species and named it. This is usually and most correctly via a scientific publication or journal. The date of this publication or the name is often given in more formal literature.

Our example was described by Carl Linnaeus, a Swedish naturalist, in 1758. He is referred to in some descriptions as Linné (a name attributed to himself after receiving a knighthood). Linnaeus is the only author whose name can be abbreviated to 'L' (L.1758), and this prefix is used in this book when species described by Linnaeus are included.

Within the phylum Mollusca, Charonia tritonis is classified as follows:

phylum	mollusca
Class	Gastropoda
Subclass	Prosobranchia
Order	Mesogastropoda
Super family	Tonnoidea
Family	Ranellidae
Subfamily	Cymatiinae
Genus	Charonia
Species	tritonis

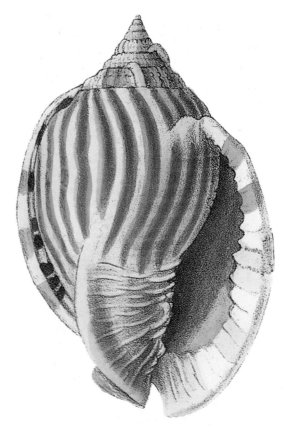

above: This fine example of a handpainted lithograph is taken from a plate in Reeve's Conchologia Iconica, 1848. The shell depicted is Phalium strigatum.

Related genera are placed within a family, although some families contain only one genus, for example Haliotidae, genus Haliotis. Large families such as Muricidae contain numerous genera. Similar or related families are, in turn, placed within super families; then comes the order, occasionally the subclass, and finally the largest category is the class.

CARL LINNAEUS
A Swedish naturalist, Carl Linnaeus, took up the challenge of tackling classification. In the 10th edition of his momentous work, Systema Naturae, published in 1758, he carefully listed and described every animal and plant, including seashells, known to him, using two Latin names for each species. For the first time in history, a uniform and concise system of nomenclature for natural things had been formulated but the binomial system, as it was named, was not widely accepted until the late 18th and early 19th centuries. The common names were slow to disappear from scientific publications and it is perhaps suprising and interesting to note that shell dealers and collectors were among the slowest to adopt the system that they considered too 'revolutionary' and 'unnecessary.'

The biology of molluscs

The gastropods are a large and diverse class that live in almost every conceivable environment, from high-tide levels to the dark depths of the ocean floor. But the majority, and certainly the most colourful and attractive, inhabit varying substrates in shallow waters relatively close to the shore, where all manner of marine life is to be found in great variety and abundance. Purple Sea Snails (Janthinidae) live pelagic lives floating on the surface of the ocean far from land.

General anatomy

The heads are usually well-developed, and comprise one or two pairs of tentacles, often carrying highly developed eyes, that can recognize light, darkness and shape. The foot is strong and muscular and is used primarily as an organ of locomotion. In numerous species a structure known as the operculum is grown on the rear portion of the foot. The operculum can be calcareous, corneus or horny, and can often be ornamented and colourful. It serves to close the aperture like a kind of door after the animal has withdrawn into its shell. In the Strombidae and Xenophoridae it is an aid to movement or can also be used as a weapon. In the Conidae, the operculum is very small and virtually useless – known as degenerate.

Gastropods have a heart, arteries and blood sinuses. The nervous system is restricted to simple 'touch organs' situated on the mantle surface, foot and tentacles.

Gastropods have gills, but respiration can also take place in and through the mantle, but only in a small number of species. The majority possess a trunk-like siphon and through this water is conducted to the gills.

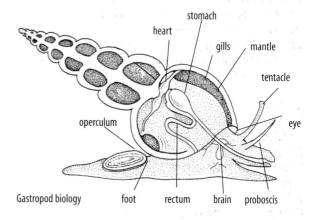

Gastropod biology

Bivalves

The bivalve shell consists of two halves, which are constructed in layers laid down by the mantle. They are joined together by a rubbery connection known as the ligament, and there is also a hinge structure with interlocking teeth, some simple, others rather complex. Classification and grouping of bivalves is often arranged by this hinge and teeth structuring.

The shapes of the valves vary considerably. When both valves are identical both in shape and size, they are referred to as being equal. Some species have gaping valves, others overlap and yet others have convex upper valves and virtually flat lower ones.

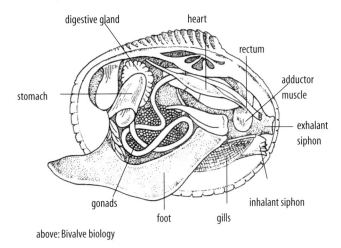

above: Bivalve biology

The bivalve body

The soft inner parts are enclosed on both sides by two large mantle lobes and these also secrete the shell-making material. No species possesses a head or radula, but some scallops and thorny oysters have light-sensitive 'eyes' situated around the mantle margins. All species possess a heart and circulatory system, and digestive organs.

The gills, which are situated within the mantle cavity, act as food filters for those species that feed on plankton and other suspended organisms, and are drawn in on the respiratory current by beating hair-like cilia in the cavity. A portion of the mantle of most bivalves is drawn out at the posterior into two siphons, one of these inhales water, while the other exhales. These can be retracted in order to close the shell. Generally the longer the siphons the deeper the shell lives in the substrate; in some cases, the siphons may be up to twice as long as the actual shell.

Oxygen is taken up by means of the mantle, the gills having little to do with respiration. The exhalent siphon is responsible for carrying away waste products.

Bivalves close their shells by means of strong adductor muscles and many species have two of these. Scars or impressions of the muscles can be observed on the valve's inner walls and are used as an aid in identification. The rubbery ligament situated close to the umbones (where the young shell commenced growth) has the opposite effect to the muscles, tending to push the valves apart. It is these opposing forces that enable the shell to open and close at will.

The shape of the foot varies according to whether it is used for creeping, burrowing or for attachment by byssus threads. It can be described as axe, tongue or worm like. In free-swimming and sessile species, the size of the foot is much reduced.

Immature shells, or those of primitive families, such as ark shells, move by slowly creeping over substrate, but most burrow in sand or mud with the help of the foot.

Cephalopods

Although this is an order which contains groups such as the octopus and squid, we are primarily concerned with the families Nautilidae and Argonautidae.

With few exceptions, the sexes are separate. There is no free-swimming larval or veliger stage; the embryo emerges fully developed from its egg.

The head and foot are united and there are gills and highly developed sensory organs. All members of this order are carnivorous and have long suckered tentacles and with these the animal seizes its prey, tearing at it with a powerful parrot-like beak.

The chambered nautilus has a large coiled shell with sealed internal chambers in a perfect spiral, each being larger than the preceding one. A central tube, the siphuncle, connects these chambers. A kind of nitrogenous gas passes through this tube and, together with an amount of fluid, creates buoyancy for mobility. By varying the amounts of these two substances, the shell can rise or submerge at will; shells, however, rarely ever come to the surface of the water.

Scaphopods

These uniquely shaped molluscs, with their hollow, tube-like and tapering shells, live buried in sand with the narrow, posterior end of the shell projecting just above the surface. The foot is situated at the opposite end and can be used to draw the animal deeper into the substrate. They possess no eyes but have a large radula.

Because they have no true gills, they breathe by inhaling water; this passes over the folds of the mantle lining, which is modified to form a tube. There are separate sexes. The embryonic form consists of two minute valves; these fuse together to form the tube-like shape and the mantle produces the shell as it grows in size.

Polyplacophora

These are fairly primitive molluscs, possessing a unique flexible shell comprised of eight plates or pieces which can be tightly coiled when attacked or when removed from rocks. The foot is powerful and is extremely difficult to remove once attached to a rock. Within its mantle cavity are the gills and sexual and excretory organs. Some species have tactile organs and primitive 'eyes' which are situated in cavities on the exposed parts of the shell. The chitons breathe by lifting part of the encircling girdle to take in water, which then passes over the gill.

All have a well-developed radula, which is used to tear at algae and other vegetable matter. The sexes are separate, and although a few species have a veliger stage, most young shells remain under the mother until they are able to fend for themselves.

Monoplacophora

This is an ancient order long considered extinct since the Devonian period. However, in May 1952, the Dutch research vessel Galathea off Costa Rica, fished up a 'living fossil.' A shell resembling a circular flat limpet was taken from a muddy substrate at 3,590 m (11,850 ft and this long-lost mollusc, a truly amazing and sensational find, was named Neopilina galatheae. Since that time, several other species have been discovered and named. The soft parts are segmented and there are gills, mouth and excretory, but no visual, organs. Research continues on these primitive and extremely rare shells.

Habitat

Seashells are able to inhabit almost any environment where water can offer an adequate supply of food, but the majority of species, and certainly the most highly coloured and patterned shells, exist in shallow waters. For the purposes of this book, the sea and seashore can be divided up into the following zones or areas:

Intertidal The area between the highest and lowest tides, also often referred to as the littoral zone. Some species also occupy the area above the high-tide line, known as the splash zone.

Sub-tidal Also known as the shallow-water zone, this includes waters below the low-tide line, coral reefs and continental shelves.

Abyssal Also called the deep-water zone, this describes the lightless regions, down to the ocean floor.

Many species thrive in sand or in muddy habitats, and burrowing shells such as olives, mitres and numerous bivalves, find sandy substrates ideal. Mangrove swamps also provide a food-rich habitat for numerous species, such as horn shells and mud creepers.

On rocky coasts, where rougher conditions prevail, you will find species with strongly constructed shells (limpets, top shells and chitons) that are adapted to cling to rock faces and boulders without being washed away. Other, less sturdy, species tend to live under rocks and slabs, or in rocky crevices.

Coral reefs are an ideal habitat for numerous species of mollusc, and here the majority of the highly coloured and attractive shells are found, mostly in tropical areas.

So-called pelagic species live on or near the surface of the sea, away from shores and land attached to a 'raft' of bubbles. In deep water or the abyssal zones, other well-adapted species exist; these are often thin-walled whitish or mostly colourless shells.

Collecting and cleaning shells

Conchology is a broad enough subject to encompass people of all ages and all levels of commitment from amateurs to scientists. Some people collect shells simply because they appreciate natural objects; others because they derive an artistic pleasure in their varied shapes and colours, while for others collecting becomes almost an obsession.

It is fashionable nowadays to specialize in one group or family, or in certain types of shell, perhaps because a more comprehensive collection would consume too much space or cover too broad a field for detailed study. Cowries are the most popular group, closely followed by cones, volutes and murex species. Little display space is required for cowries, and they offer a wide variety of pattern and colour. They are relatively easy to collect in the wild, and the majority can be bought for affordable prices.

Some collectors take an active interest in very tiny adult shells, known as 'micro-shells,' which are perhaps no more than 1 cm (K in) long at maturity. Another fascination to collectors is the collecting of abnormalities, or freaks. These variations from the normal are most sought after by collectors and can command high prices.

Cleaning shells

Shells purchased from dealers normally require no cleaning other than a periodic dusting or a wash in warm soapy water. Grubby specimens have even been known to benefit from a cycle in the dishwasher. Beached, faded or dull shells respond to a light rub with baby oil. This can be applied with a finger or, in the case of spinose shells, with a soft brush, and the excess wiped away with a tissue.

Live-collected shells must be cleaned of their inhabitants. Sometimes, of course, these will be edible, but in other cases a period in the deep freezer will cause the contents to fall away from the inner surface, facilitating their removal with forceps or wire.

Once the soft parts have been dealt with, it may be desirable to remove the periostracum. Place the specimen in a solution of household bleach and water for a few hours; the skin will either dissolve completely or can be gently brushed away.

Stubborn areas may require a longer period of soaking and stronger bleach solution.

Exterior encrustations can cause problems, and I have encountered numerous methods of removing hard lime encrustations and other marine debris. A wire brush can be used with care on solidly built shells which have
a non-glossy surface; other methods entail careful 'picking' with pins or forceps, or gently tapping with a small blunt instrument.

Shells that have coarse ornamentation and are dull or have a chalky appearance respond very well to a second or two's dip in a weak solution of hydrochloric acid. Although this method is frowned upon by some experts, I have found that when it is used with due care excellent results can be obtained with some species, like those of Murex, Pecten and Spondylus. Often the full potential of colour and pattern can be realized only with this apparently extreme treatment.

Once a shell has totally lost its colour, little or nothing can be done to retrieve its former glory. Seashells, like other cherished collectable items, have to be safeguarded against external elements, especially sunlight, which can seriously fade the colour of a shell in a relatively short period of time. Specimens are best housed indoors away from direct sunlight.

Displaying shells

However you have collected your shells, they deserve to be displayed to their best advantage. A growing collection will eventually need to be moved away from shelves or coffee tables, where they are open to damage from bright natural light, and into cases or specially designed drawers.

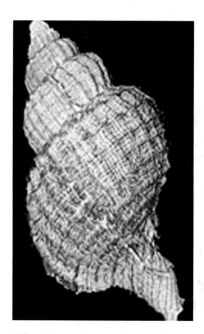

With periostracum

Without periostracum

Class
Gastropoda

At least three-quarters of the world's molluscs are included in this, the largest class, and approximately half the species are marine. The snails are soft-bodied, with tentacles, eyes, a mantle and a broad, flat foot. The visceral mass where most internal organs are situated is contained in a one-piece, usually coiled, hard shell. The majority of gastropods are mobile, highly active creatures. There are perhaps between 20,000 and 30,000 described species and these include such well-known families as limpets, cowries, murex, cones and olives.

SUPER FAMILY
PLEUROTOMARIOIDEA

FAMILY
PLEUROTOMARIIDAE
(Slit Shells)

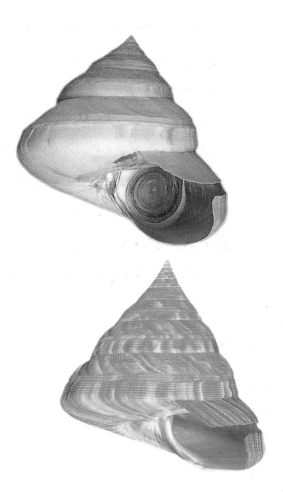

This is an ancient group of molluscs, its ancestors dating back to early Cambrian times. The 16 or so surviving species – all vegetarians – occur in very deep waters, some down to 600 m (1,980 ft), in areas as widespread as China and Caribbean Seas and off the coast of Southern Africa. They are therefore considered rare shells (indeed, apart from fossil evidence, the first recent species was only discovered in the mid-19th century in the Caribbean), and are seldom seen in amateur collections. The shells are generally rounded and conical, relatively large – *Pleurotomania rumplii* can reach over 20 cm (8 in) – and all have the characteristic anal slit through which waste water escapes, and a horny rounded operculum. There are three genera: *Entemnotrochus, Perotrochus* and *Mikadotrochus*.

Perotrochus · Hirasei

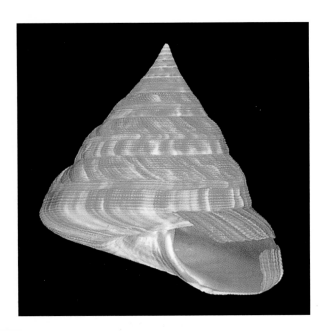

Description

One of the more common species from this family, this is probably also the most attractive, having a thick heavy shell with rounded rather flat shoulders. Spiral cording and beading ornamentation give a latticed effect. The umbilicus area is highly nacreous and the colouration generally ranges from pale to deep orange red in the form of haphazard diagonal streaking on a cream background. This species, along with others fished in similar waters, was once known to fishermen as the 'millionaire shell.'

Other common names:
  The Emperor's Slit Shell
Author of the species, form or variety:
  Pilsbry
Date of publication:
  1903
Average size of mature shell:
  10 cm (4 in)
Locality:
  Taiwan and Japan
Habitat depth:
  Between 150 and 500 m (495–1,650 ft)
Availability:
  Rare

Perotrochus · Africana

Description

Compared to P. hirasei, this is a very light, thin shell, less conical and more angular. It is pale beige or orange in colour and has minute spiral cording. Two thin spiral bands of a deeper orange wind back and upwards on the shoulders of each whorl, running from the rear of the slit to the apex of the shell.

Other common names:
  African Slit Shell
Author of the species, form or variety:
  Tomlin
Date of publication:
  1948
Average size of mature shell:
  13 cm (5 in)
Locality:
  South Africa
Habitat depth:
  Between 150 and 500 m (495–1,650 ft)
Availability:
  Rare

SUPER FAMILY
PLEUROTOMARIOIDEA

FAMILY
HALIOTIDAE
(Abalones)

A large family, numbering perhaps 100 recognized named species, abalones are also commonly known as ormers or sea ears in various localities. They are a valuable seafood and several species – notably the larger abalones of California – have been farmed for lucrative commercial markets. The shape is fairly constant, being flat, with little evidence of a spire, and either rounded or oval. All possess a series of holes on the body whorl through which water and waste are passed. All interiors are highly nacreous and iridescent, and can be very colourful. Most show evidence of a central muscle scar in the interior. Their habitat ranges from low-tide zones – in shallow water attached firmly to rocks – down to, on occasions, some hundreds of feet. There is one genus: *Haliotis.*

Haliotis · Mariae

Description

Strong thickened rounded ridges are the major characteristic on the exterior or dorsum of this shell. The colouration ranges from beige to pale red, with a delicate pinkish green pearly interior. Specimens are often encrusted with marine deposits and small barnacles.

Other common names:
  Marie's Abalone
Author of the species, form or variety:
  Gray
Date of publication:
  1831
Average size of mature shell:
  10 cm (4 in)
Locality:
  Oman
Habitat depth:
  Extends to about 25 m (83 ft)
Availability:
  Uncommon

Haliotis · Emmae

Description

A pretty little shell, this is similar to *H. scalaris*, but the dorsum is less sculptured. The holes are raised and rounded, and there are spiral ridges. It is a pale pink, with large, dull reddish brown radial patches. This specimen was found off Port Lincoln.

Other common names:
  Emma's Abalone
Author of the species, form or variety:
  Gray
Date of publication:
  1846
Average size of mature shell:
  8 cm (3¼ in)
Locality:
  Southern Australia
Habitat depth:
  Extends to about 25 m (83 ft)
Availability:
  Uncommon

Haliotis · Asinina

Haliotis · Asinina

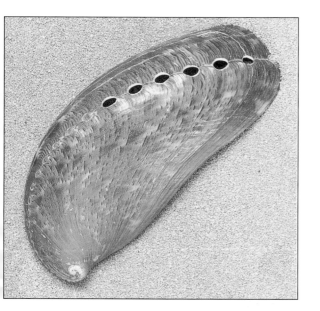

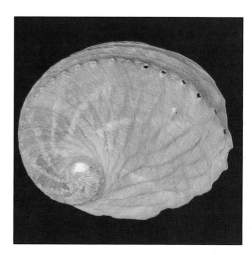

Description

This curved, smooth shell is elongated in shape and is aptly named. The exterior is a pale olive green, enlivened with odd splashes of brown. The interior is white with hints of green. For the size of the shell, the holes are large. The dorsum is sometimes commercially polished to show the fine nacreous layers below.

Description

H. rubber is a very beautiful large abalone with a pale red dorsum. The interior nacre is primarily white, and features wide radiating flattened ridges. The spire is often eroded to show the lower layers of nacre. A shallow-water dweller.

Other common names:
  Ass's Ear Abalone
Author of the species, form or variety:
  L.
Date of publication:
  1758
Average size of mature shell:
  10 cm (4 in)
Locality:
  Central Indo-Pacific
Habitat depth:
  Extends to about 25 m (83 ft)
Availability:
  Abundant

Other common names:
  Not known
Author of the species, form or variety:
  Leach
Date of publication:
  1814
Average size of mature shell:
  15 cm (6 in)
Locality:
  Southern Australia
Habitat depth:
  Extends to about 25 m (83 ft)
Availability:
  Common

SUPER FAMILY
FISSURELLOIDEA

FAMILY
FISSURELLIDAE
(Keyhole Limpets)

This is a large family of primitive snails with shells which are generally rounded to ovate in shape. They have a worldwide distribution, including the coldest seas, inhabiting rocky coastlines and coral below the low-tide areas. None possesses an operculum. All are egg-laying vegetarians. Most have the natural hole at the top of the shell, though a few have a marginal slit or indentation at the front. The interior of most species is porcellaneous. An interesting group, this promotes little interest among amateur collectors, perhaps because the shells are comparatively dull and ordinary in appearance.

Fissurella · Aperta

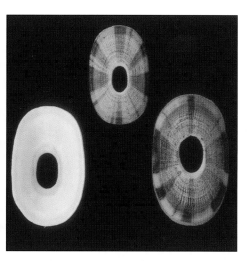

Description

This endemic shell lives on and under rocks in intertidal waters. The small but solid shell is elongated and features a large hole in relation to its overall size. The colouration is beige to pink, overlaid with fine radial lines and rays. The margin is white, giving the appearance of two edges. The interior is pure white.

Other common names:
   Double-edged Keyhole Limpet
Author of the species, form or variety:
   Sowerby
Date of publication:
   1825
Average size of mature shell:
   3 cm (3 1/4 in)
Locality:
   South Africa
Habitat depth:
   Extends to about 25 m (83 ft)
Availability:
   Common

Fissurella · Maxima

Description

The large, heavy shell is mainly cream, with wide red-to-brown rays, radiating from the slightly ovate hole. The surface is ridged with growth lines. The interior is white, with a cream margin edged with reddish brown. There is a finely ridged horseshoe-shaped muscle scar. F. maxima inhabits rock reefs.

Other common names:
   Giant Keyhole Limpet
Author of the species, form or variety:
   Sowerby
Date of publication:
   1835
Average size of mature shell:
   12 cm (4 3/4 in)
Locality:
   Western South America
Habitat depth:
   Extends to about 25 m (83 ft)
Availability:
   Common

Fissurella · Nodosa

Description

Heavily nodulose radiating ridges and a figure-of-eight hole are the main characteristics of this species. The shell is ovate, with a relatively high spire. The interior is white, with fine incised grooves radiating from the hole to the margins. Found on rocks in the intertidal zone.

Other common names:
  Knobbed Keyhole Limpet
Author of the species, form or variety:
  Born
Date of publication:
  1778
Average size of mature shell:
  3 cm (1¼ in)
Locality:
  Florida and West Indies
Habitat depth:
  Extends to about 25 m (83 ft)
Availability:
  Common

Fissurella ·Peruviana

Description

A small rounded shell with a conical pointed spire it has relatively straight sides and is pale crimson in colour with wide dark greyish brown rays. The small hole is edged in cream. The interior is white with a crimson margin.

Other common names:
  Peruvian Keyhole Limpet
Author of the species, form or variety:
  Lamarck
Date of publication:
  1822
Average size of mature shell:
  2.5 cm (1 in)
Locality:
  Western South America
Habitat depth:
  Extends to about 25 m (83 ft)
Availability:
  Common

SUPER FAMILY
PATELLOIDEA

FAMILIES
ACMAEIDAE and LOTTIIDAE
(True Limpets)

There are small biological differences between these two families and the Patellidae, but the collector need only consider the appearance of the shells. The shapes are all somewhat similar, being rounded, oval or regular. However, the interiors of these two families are porcellaneous and often colourful, whereas the Patellidae tend to have nacreous and iridescent interiors. The main genus of Acmaeidae is Acmaea, while Lottis and Scurria belong to *Lottiidae*.

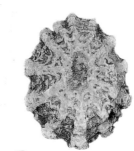

Lottia • Gigantea

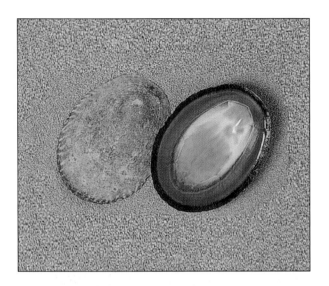

Description

A flat, ovate and rather light species, the giant owl limpet inhabits on-shore rocks near the high-tide line. Beneath the dorsum, which is usually encrusted, there is a maculated patterning which can often be noticed at the margin. The interior bears a white or pale blue oval scar and the surround is a uniform dark to mid-toned brown. The margin edge has a thick black band.

Other common names:
   Giant Owl Limpet
Author of the species, form or variety:
   Sowerby
Date of publication:
   1834
Average size of mature shell:
   7 cm (2¾ in)
Locality:
   California to Mexico
Habitat depth:
   Extends to about 25 m (83 ft)
Availability:
   Common

Patelloida • Alticostata

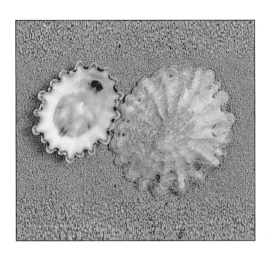

Description

Widespread on intertidal rocks, its main food source is the marine plant, ulva. The dorsum of this small but solid limpet bears about 18-20 rounded moderate radial ribs between which, on younger less-encrusted specimens, are fine grey spinal lines. Interiors vary slightly between white and off-white and have a grey or pale brown central scar. The more colourful shells are edged with black between the interior marginal crenulation.

Other common names:
   High white Limpet
Author of the species, form or variety:
   Menke
Date of publication:
   1851
Average size of mature shell:
   2.5 cm (1 in)
Locality:
   Western Central America
Habitat depth:
   Extends to about 25 m (83 ft)
Availability:
   Common

Scurria • Mesoleuca

Scurria • Variabilis

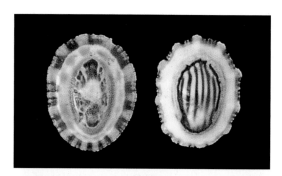

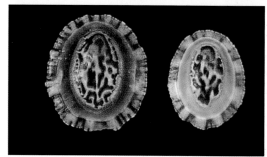

Description

A thin, rather fragile, flat limpet with fine radial dorsal ridges and white dashes on a mud brown background. The interior colour is pale duck-egg blue with a grey central scar flecked with orange. The margin is edged with blue and brown at the extremities. An intertidal rock dweller.

Description

The author is unknown but this shell had to be included due to its sheer prettiness! This tiny species has a dirty greyish brown dorsum which is usually encrusted. The central scar area inside is highly attractive and variable in patterning – several are shown here. Brown, beige or white and even pale blue rims occur, with short radial lines and dashes on the margin.

Other common names:
  Half-white Limpet
Author of the species, form or variety:
  Unknown
Date of publication:
  Unknown
Average size of mature shell:
  2 cm (¾ in)
Locality:
  Chile
Habitat depth:
  Extends to about 25 m (83 ft)
Availability:
  Uncommon

Other common names:
  Variable Scurria
Author of the species, form or variety:
  Unknown
Date of publication:
  Unknown
Average size of mature shell:
  2 cm (¾ in)
Locality:
  Chile
Habitat depth:
  Extends to about 25 m (83 ft)
Availability:
  Uncommon

SUPER FAMILY
PATELLOIDEA

FAMILIES
ACMAEIDAE and LOTTIIDAE
(True Limpets)

A large group, with limpet-like, flat-to-conical shells possessing no hole at the apex, they tend to move about at night time and return to their sites at dawn, when they become firmly attached to rocky surfaces. All are vegetarian and none possess an operculum. Patellidae are divided into two subfamilies, Patellinae and Nacellinae, of which there are several genera and subgenera, notably Patella, Nacella and Cellana. The shapes of limpets show clearly how well they are adapted to their harsh environment, their more or less flat shape and their ability to cling tightly to rocks enabling them to withstand fierce wave action and strong currents.

Lottia · Gigantea

Description

A flat, ovate and rather light species, the giant owl limpet inhabits on-shore rocks near the high-tide line. Beneath the dorsum, which is usually encrusted, there is a maculated patterning, which can often be noticed at the margin. The interior bears a white of pale blue oval scar and the surround is a uniform dark to mid-toned brown. The margin edge has a thick black band.

Other common names:
  Giant Owl Limpet
Author of the species, form or variety:
  Sowerby
Date of publication:
  1834
Average size of mature shell:
  7 cm (2 3/4 in)
Locality:
  California to Mexico
Habitat depth:
  Extends to about 25 m (83 ft)
Availability:
  Common

Patella · Concolour

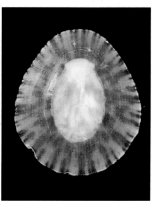

Description

As the common name suggests, this is an extremely variable species – not in shape, but in colour and patterning. The dorsum generally bears fine radial ridges, sometimes obscured by deposits of marine debris. The interior is nacreous and prettily patterned with pale and dark radial dots and dashes. The overall colour ranges from off-white to deep yellow or orange. There is a faint central scar mark. There are several named varieties, with differing patterns and colours. This species is found on intertidal rocks.

Other common names:
  Variable Limpet
Author of the species, form or variety:
  Krauss
Date of publication:
  1848
Average size of mature shell:
  4 cm (1½ in)
Locality:
  South Africa
Habitat depth:
  Extends to about 25 m (83 ft)
Availability:
  Common

Patella · Ferruginea

Patella · Granatina

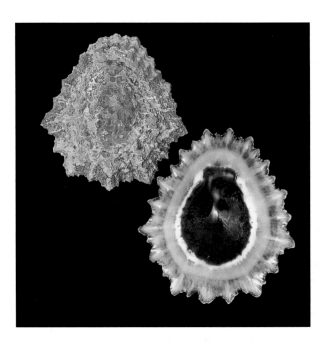

Description

An elongated or ovate species, its dorsum bears coarse, sometimes nodulose, ribs that extend to the margin, giving a crenulated effect. Somewhat convex when viewed from the side, the shell has a pale grey porecellaneous interior, bearing a prominent oval scar; the edges of the crenulated margin are brown. Found on intertidal rocks.

Description

This has a rather stout shell, with sharply angular radial ridges. On mature specimens the dorsum is usually partly eroded away due to the conditions of its habitat. The colour ranges from grey to beige. Interior colours vary, although there is always a large dark brown central scar. Some are a pale yellowish green with flecks and flashes of grey at the margins, while others show a white horseshoe mark and are edged with deep yellow or blue. All in all, a very attractive species.

Other common names:
  Ribbed Limpet
Author of the species, form or variety:
  Gmelin
Date of publication:
  1791
Average size of mature shell:
  7.5 cm (3 in)
Locality:
  Mediterranean
Habitat depth:
  Extends to about 25 m (83 ft)
Availability:
  Common

Other common names:
  Sandpaper Limpet
Author of the species, form or variety:
  L.
Date of publication:
  1758
Average size of mature shell:
  8 cm (3¼ in)
Locality:
  South Africa
Habitat depth:
  Extends to about 25 m (83 ft)
Availability:
  Common

Patella · Granularis

Description

This limpet occurs on all rocky South African shorelines. As with many molluscs in this area, collecting may be limited to only 15 specimens per day. The shell is smallish but stout, with radiating ribs, sometimes with sharp nodules. Large shells can be eroded on the spire. The interior bears a large brown central scar on a background which is usually a pale blue grey. There is a thick dark grey or black marginal rim, indented with shallow grooves.

Other common names:
  Granular Limpet
Author of the species, form or variety:
  L.
Date of publication:
  1758
Average size of mature shell:
  6 cm (2½ in)
Locality:
  South Africa
Habitat depth:
  Extends to about 25 m (83 ft)
Availability:
  Abundant

Patella · Tabularis

Description

This is the largest of all African limpets. It is ovate, and the dorsum has many moderate-to-coarse angled ribs extending radially to form a crenulated margin. The shell, when not encrusted, ranges in colour from a dull pale to bright red. Large specimens bear sponge or worm holes on or near the apex. The interior is porcellaneous white. Younger small shells have a pale red rim around the margin.

Other common names:
  Tabular Limpet
Author of the species, form or variety:
  Krauss
Date of publication:
  1848
Average size of mature shell:
  13 cm (5 in)
Locality:
  South Africa
Habitat depth:
  Extends to about 25 m (83 ft)
Availability:
  Common

SUPER FAMILY
TROCHOIDEA

FAMILY
TROCHIDAE
(Top Shells)

The hundreds of species which make up the Trochidae are divided biologically into subfamilies, including Monodontinae, Gibbulinae Calliostomatinae and Trochinae. These are further divided into many genera, some of which are named here. The Trochidae enjoy worldwide distribution and habitats vary from shallow rock pools down to the abyssal zones. Most species are herbivores, some feeding on sponges. The shapes often determine habitat – the high-spired species usually dwell in calmer sheltered waters, whereas the flatter, low-spired shells live in areas where rough seas are prevalent. Virtually all are conical or top-shaped, however. All possess horny operculae.

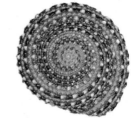

Cantharidus · Opalus

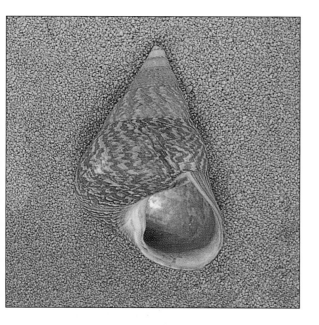

Description

A tall shell with a large aperture, this has slightly rounded whorls and is pale grey overlaid with dull reddish brown axial zigzag lines. The nacre below the outer shell covering – and within the aperture – is of a wonderful greenish blue. Lives on seaweeds in fairly deep water.

Other common names:
Opal Top Shell
Author of the species, form or variety:
Martyn
Date of publication:
1784
Average size of mature shell:
3 cm (1¼ in)
Locality:
New Zealand
Habitat depth:
Between 25 and 150 m (83–495 ft)
Availability:
Common

Monodonta · Labio

Description

Thick and heavy, this species has a low spire and a large rounded body whorl. There are several rows of incised ridges on each whorl and the pale greenish brown is overlaid with squares and patches of dark brown and grey. The columella supports two large white 'teeth.' The interior of the aperture is chalky white, has strong lirae and a thin narcreous edge.

Other common names:
Toothed Monodont
Author of the species, form or variety:
Von Salis
Date of publication:
1793
Average size of mature shell:
1 cm (⅜ in)
Locality:
Mediterranean
Habitat depth:
Between 25 and 150 m (83–495 ft)
Availability:
Common

Cittarium · Pica

Description

A well-known and popular edible species, it inhabits sub-tidal rocky areas and is thick and heavy, with rounded whorls and a large gaping aperture. The umbilicus is open. The background colouring is white and the entire shell is covered with thick black wavy axial lines. The operculum is horny and circular.

Other common names:
  Magpie Shell
Author of the species, form or variety:
  L.
Date of publication:
  1758
Average size of mature shell:
  7.5 cm (3 in)
Locality:
  Caribbean
Habitat depth:
  Extends to about 25 m (83 ft)
Availability:
  Common

Tegula · Regina

Description

This has a large dark gray shell with four to six overlapping horls bearing wavy exial ribs. The aperture is nacreous and stained with deep yellow and there is a vivid orange spiral band around the umbilicus. The operculum is circular and horny. It is generally a difficult shell to rid of marine deposits. The apex is often worn and can show worm holes and other signs of damage.

Other common names:
  Regal Top
Author of the species, form or variety:
  Gmelin
Date of publication:
  1791
Average size of mature shell:
  4 cm (1⅜ in)
Locality:
  South Africa
Habitat depth:
  Extends to about 25 m (83 ft)
Availability:
  Common

Maurea · Punctulata

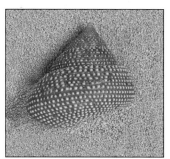

Description

A short, rather squat species, with a large rounded body whorl, it bears many rows of fine spiral cording. The background colour is beige or mid-brown and the cords bear alternate white and brown dots and dashes. These specimens were found on rocks at low tide, Mahanga Beach, New Zealand.

Description

This tiny species had a low spire and a large rounded body whorl. The background colouring is beige grey with mottled patches and spiral dots of pale brown to deep grey. The suture is incised. The umbilicus is open and relatively large and the internal nacre is a deep blue green. These specimens were collected in marine grass in shallow water in Malta.

Other common names:
  Punctate Maurea
Author of the species, form or variety:
  Martyn
Date of publication:
  1784
Average size of mature shell:
  4 cm (1½ in)
Locality:
  New Zealand
Habitat depth:
  Extends to about 25 m (83 ft)
Availability:
  Uncommon

Other common names:
  Ardens Top
Author of the species, form or variety:
  Von Salis
Date of publication:
  1793
Average size of mature shell:
  1 cm (⅜ in)
Locality:
  Mediterranean
Habitat depth:
  Extends to about 25 m (83 ft)
Availability:
  Common

Calliostoma · Monile

Description

This is a pretty and delicate little shell with straight sides and a tall spire. There are minute spiral striae on the whorls. The colour is pale beige with a dominant band running above the sutures of pale purple squares and 'flames' on white. It lives on sponges in shallow water.

Other common names:
Monile Top
Author of the species, form or variety:
Reeve
Date of publication:
1863
Average size of mature shell:
2 cm (¾ in)
Locality:
Western Australia
Habitat depth:
Extends to about 25 m (83 ft)
Availability:
Uncommon

Tectus · Triserialis

Description

A very elegant, tall and narrow species, *T. triserialis* has slightly rounded shoulders. The 13 or so whorls bear several broken rows of blunt white nodules set against a background which is generally pale green or brown. The base is white with fine spiral grooves.

Other common names:
Tall Top
Author of the species, form or variety:
Lamarck
Date of publication:
1822
Average size of mature shell:
5.5 cm (2¼ in)
Locality:
Philippines
Habitat depth:
Extends to about 25 m (83 ft)
Availability:
Uncommon

Gaza · Superba

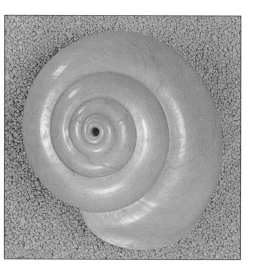

Trochus · Dentatus

Description

A very light fragile species, rounded and depressed, its shell is much desired by collectors. The gazas are a small, rare genus and all appear to be thin shelled with the pearly interior showing through. *G. superba* is a pale lime green with gold and pink undertones. A nacreous parietal wall partly covers the otherwise wide umbilicus. This specimen was dredged at a depth of 500 m (1,650 ft) off Pensacola, Florida.

Description

Solid and fairly heavy, this has about 10 whorls, the sides of which are slightly concave. Prominent extended nodules occur on the lower part of each whorl, overlapping the suture. The pale beige or pink shell is often heavily encrusted. The base is mainly chalky white. It feeds on algae on reef flats in shallow water.

Other common names:
  Superb Gaza
Author of the species, form or variety:
  Dall
Date of publication:
  1881
Average size of mature shell:
  4 cm (1½ in)
Locality:
  Gulf of Mexico and West Indies
Habitat depth:
  Between 150 and 500 m
  (495–1,650 ft)
Availability:
  Rare

Other common names:
  Toothed Top
Author of the species, form or variety:
  Forskal
Date of publication:
  1775
Average size of mature shell:
  5.5 cm (2¼ in)
Locality:
  Red Sea and Indian Ocean
Habitat depth:
  25 m (83 ft)
Availability:
  Common

SUPER FAMILY
TROCHOIDEA
FAMILY
TURBINIDAE
(Turban Shells)

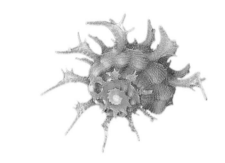

The turban shells are a large family comprising several hundred species which are divided into three subfamilies, Angariinae (Dolphin Shells), Turbininae (True Turbans) and Astraeinae (Star Shells). The Angariinae are a small group of relatively large shells with spiral ornamentation. Some have long curved spines. Angaria is the only genus and all are collectors' items. The turbans tend to have solid top-shaped shells with large body whorls and apertures. Genera include Turbo, Ninella and Lunella. The Astraeinae are popular and varied collectors' shells which are generally conical to top-shaped with flat bases, often highly ornamented with long spines. The main genera are Astraea, Bolina and Guildfordia. Most species of the family are vegetarian and usually prefer warm shallow water.

Angaria · Delphinulus Aculaeta

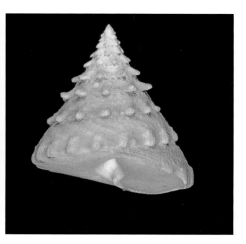

Description

Another very variable but attractive form of *A. delphinilus*. The specimen shown was fished 10 m of water at Sinabe, Okinawa and shoes typical characteristics of a flat spire, and an enlarged and very spinose body whorl. The colour is exquisite, consisting of pale red and pink, with golden tipped spines.

Other common names:
  Aculeate Delphinula
Author of the species, form or variety:
  Reeve
Date of publication:
  1842
Average size of mature shell:
  3 cm (1¼ in)
Locality:
  Japan and Philippines
Habitat depth:
  Between 25 and150 m (83–495 ft)
Availability:
  Uncommon

Angaria · Delphinulus melanacantha

Description

A thick, highly spinose species, it has a flat spire with virtually only an enlarged body whorl which swings out and drops downwards revealing an open and spinose umbilicus. The sides and top of the whorl bear black spines of varying length, while those on the shoulder project outwards and upwards, occasionally touching each other. The background colour is a pale greyish purple. The aperture is highly nacreous.

Other common names:
  Imperial Delphinula
Author of the species, form or variety:
  Reeve
Date of publication:
  1842
Average size of mature shell:
  6 cm (2½ in)
Locality:
  Philippines
Habitat depth:
  Between 25 and150 m (83–495 ft)
Availability:
  Common

Angaria · Nodulosa

Description

Some people consider this a variety of *A. delphinulus*, but I will treat it as a species in its own right. A large, virtually continuous body whorl radiates from a flat or depressed spire (when viewed from above) . There are several rounded or scaled nodules, both on the shoulder and below the whorl, and a delicate spiral beading of fine red dots on a pale pink background. This shell was collected at a depth of 66 feet (20 m) off Sinabe, Okinawa.

Other common names:
  Knobbed Delphinula
Author of the species, form or variety:
  Reeve
Date of publication:
  1846
Average size of mature shell:
  4 cm (1½ in)
Locality:
  Japan
Habitat depth:
  Between 25 and150 m (83–495 ft)
Availability:
  Uncommon

Angaria · Tyria

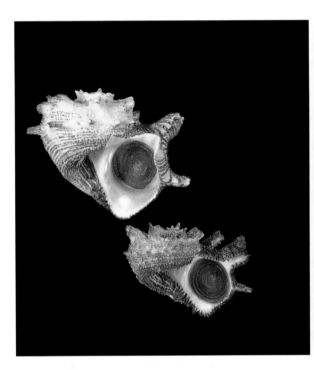

Description

Two forms of this extremely variable species are depicted here. Again, some experts would put A. tyria as yet a further form of A. delphinulus. This may well be the case, but in this instance it is being treated as a species in its own right. The smaller of the two is probably a Philippine shell, whereas the larger was fished off North-West Australia. Extremely variable.

Other common names:
  Tyria Delphinula
Author of the species, form or variety:
  Reeve
Date of publication:
  1842
Average size of mature shell:
  7 cm (2¾ in)
Locality:
  South-West Pacific and Australia
Habitat depth:
  Between 25 and150 m (83–495 ft)
Availability:
  Uncommon

Angaria · Delphinulus

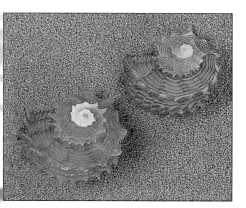

Description

This is the best-known form of the Delphinulus group. It has a flat spire, only about two whorls, and a large umbilicus. Each whorl supports many spinose spiral ridges, the spines being longer and sharper at the shoulders. Colours vary from pale pink to almost black. These specimens are from southern India.

Other common names:
Common Delphinula
Author of the species, form or variety:
L.
Date of publication:
1758
Average size of mature shell:
5 cm (2 in)
Locality:
Indo-Pacific
Habitat depth:
Between 25 and150 m (83–495 ft)
Availability:
Common

Turbo · Petholatus

Description

This beautifully patterned species is found in a wide range of colour variations. Very popular, it has proved an inspiration to artists and designers as well as lovers of natural objects. The shell is rather bulbous and stout, smooth and glossy and is covered with bands and axial streaks and 'flames' of various colours, including browns, greens and beiges. The operculum – known as a 'cat's eye' – is thick and is predominantly dark green.

Other common names:
Tapestry Turban
Author of the species, form or variety:
L.
Date of publication:
1758
Average size of mature shell:
5.5 cm (2¼ in)
Locality:
Indo-Pacific
Habitat depth:
Extends to about 25 m (83 ft)
Availability:
Common

Turbo · Radiatus

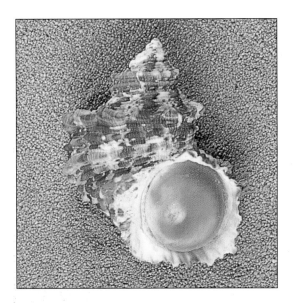

Description

T. radiatus has a moderate spire and an enlarged body
whorl and aperture, coarsely sculptured with rows of
out-turned blunt nodules – three rows per whorl. The
colour range extends from mottled beige through to
dark brown. The thick operculum is smooth. An
intertidal reef dweller.

Other common names:
  Radial Turban
Author of the species, form or variety:
  Gmelin
Date of publication:
  1791
Average size of mature shell:
  4 cm (1½ in)
Locality:
  Red Sea and Gulf of Oman
Habitat depth:
  Extends to about 25 m (83 ft)
Availability:
  Uncommon

Turbo · Reevei

Description

This species varies from *T. petholatus* by being rather
smaller and having less dramatic patterning. The
colour variations are no less vivid, however, ranging
from pale to deep orange, green and reddish brown
through to near black, many having mottling or axial
zigzag lines. The depicted specimens were collected
from the Sulu Sea.

Other common names:
  Reeve's Turban
Author of the species, form or variety:
  Philippi
Date of publication:
  1847
Average size of mature shell:
  4 cm (1½ in)
Locality:
  Philippines
Habitat depth:
  Extends to about 25 m (83 ft)
Availability:
  Common

Astraea · Heliotropium

Description

This deep-water shell is seldom obtained in pristine condition – it is usually entirely covered with lime and marine encrustations and is difficult to clean. The species was reputedly discovered on the cable of a vessel belonging to Captain Cook's fleet in the waters later to be named Cook Strait.

Other common names:
  Sunburst Star Shell
Author of the species, form or variety:
  Martyn
Date of publication:
  1784
Average size of mature shell:
  10 cm (4 in)
Locality:
  New Zealand
Habitat depth:
  Between 25 and 250 m
  (495–1,650 ft)
Availability:
  Uncommon

Australium · Calcar

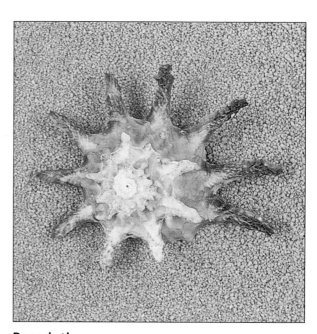

Description

Long spines sometimes protrude from the whorl periphery of this almost flat shell. The base colour is a green beige, and the slightly ovate operculum is dark green. There is fine spiral beading on the base of the shell. The aperture is nacreous. Many specimens are heavily encrusted and eroded at the apex.

Other common names:
  Philippine Star Shell
Author of the species, form or variety:
  L.
Date of publication:
  1758
Average size of mature shell:
  5 cm (2 in)
Locality:
  Philippines
Habitat depth:
  Extends to about 25 m (83 ft)
Availability:
  Common

Bolma · Aureola

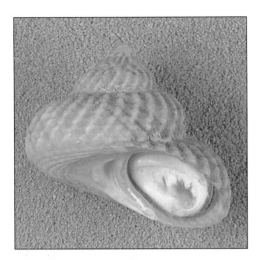

Description

Found only off Queensland in depths 0 130 ft this shell is large, with straight sides. The whorls are slightly angled at the suture. The shoulders bear a single row of short sharp spines which could project outward and elsewhere there are haphazard rows of low nodular ridges. The shell is orange brown with a pale orange and white operculum. The aperture and columella are edged in bright orange.

Other common names:
  Bridled Bolma
Author of the species, form or variety:
  Hedley
Date of publication:
  1907
Average size of mature shell:
  7.5 cm (3 in)
Locality:
  Queensland, Australia
Habitat depth:
  Between 25 and 150 m (83-495 ft)
Availability:
  Uncommon

Cookia · Sulcata

Description

One of several species possibly first discovered on the voyages of Captain James Cook of South Sea Island fame, this is a robust squat shell with a low spire. There are rows of nodulose diagonal ridges and the overall colouring is a dull beige. Many collected specimens are highly encrusted. The operculum is off-white and has the appearance of an 'ear.' An intertidal rock dweller.

Other common names:
  Captain Cook's Turban
Author of the species, form or variety:
  Gmelin
Date of publication:
  1791
Average size of mature shell:
  9 cm (3½ in)
Locality:
  New Zealand
Habitat depth:
  Extends to about 25 m (83 ft)
Availability:
  Common

Guildfordia · Triumphans

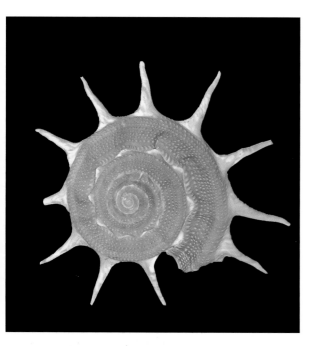

Description

Another almost flat shell with a low spire, this has long projecting spines at right angles to the body whorl and much fine spiral beading overall. The colour is a pink-toned bronze and the base is off-white to cream. The operculum is white and ovate. A collectors' favourite. It is a deep-water species.

Other common names:
  Triumphant Star
Author of the species, form or variety:
  Philippi
Date of publication:
  1841
Average size of mature shell:
  5.5 cm (2¼ in)
Locality:
  Taiwan and Japan
Habitat depth:
  Between 150 and 500 m (495–1,650 ft)
Availability:
  Common

Megastraea · Turbanica

Description

The bigger of the two species in this genus, (the other being *M. undosa*), large live specimens – over 7.5 cm (3 in) – have only been fished from deep-water kelp beds since the 1950s. Prior to this the only evidence came from dead shells and fossils. The shell has straight sides to the apex and each whorl bears rows of stunted and pronounced nodules. The colour is generally off-white, but the early whorls are often dull brick-red or pinkish. This deep-water species is popular with collectors.

Other common names:
  Turban Star Shell
Author of the species, form or variety:
  Dall
Date of publication:
  1910
Average size of mature shell:
  15 cm (6 in)
Locality:
  Southern California to Mexico
Habitat depth:
  Between 150 and 500 m (495–1,650 ft)
Availability:
  Uncommon

SUPER FAMILY
TROCHOIDEA

FAMILIES
PHASIANELLIDAE and TRICOLIIDAE
(Pheasant Shells)

These two families contain the genera *Phasianella* and *Tricolia*, but have relatively few species. The shells possess smooth exteriors which are usually colourful and patterned, the apertures being non-nacreous but porcellaneous. The operculae are chalky white, smooth and glossy. Most species are vegetarian.

Phasianella · Australis

Description

A tall, fairly narrow shell, with rounded whorls, its surface is smooth and glossy and is highly patterned. There are many variations, and the ones shown here are just a selection. The thick white operculum is almond-shaped.

Other common names:
  Australian Pheasant
Author of the species, form or variety:
  Gmelin
Date of publication:
  1791
Average size of mature shell:
  5.5 cm (2¼ in)
Locality:
  Southern Australia
Habitat depth:
  Extends to about 25 m (83 ft)
Availability:
  Common

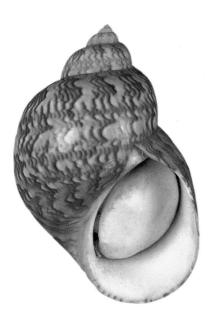

Phasianella · Ventricosa

Description

Although in texture it is identical to *P. australis*, the shape of *P. ventricosa* differs in that the spire is relatively low and the body whorl large and bulbous. Once again, patterns and colours can be extremely variable. The operculum is white and calcareous.

Other common names:
Swollen Pheasant
Author of the species, form or variety:
Swainson
Date of publication:
1822
Average size of mature shell:
4 cm (1½ in)
Locality:
Southern Australia
Habitat depth:
Extends to about 25 m (83 ft)
Availability:
Common

Tricolia · Pulla

Description

The *Tricolia* genus consists of very small shells, and you will have to inspect this particular species with an eye-glass to appreciate its beauty. It is globose, with rounded whorls and a moderate spire. The colour of this tiny gem is a rich reddish pink overlaid with tiny deeper red spots and zigzag lines. There are larger patches of cream and brown just below the suture. The neat tiny operculum is calcareous, and off-white in colour. These examples are from Sines, Portugal.

Other common names:
Red Pheasant
Author of the species, form or variety:
L.
Date of publication:
1758
Average size of mature shell:
1 cm (⅜ in)
Locality:
Mediterranean and North-East Atlantic coasts
Habitat depth:
Extends to about 25 m (83 ft)
Availability: Common

SUPER FAMILY
NERITOIDEA

FAMILY
NERITIDAE
(Nerites)

The nerites are arguably one of the less popular families. This group of smallish shells comprises only about 50 species. There are several genera and subgenera, including *Nerita, Neritina, Smaragdia* and *Theodoxus*. Nerites are able to store water within their shell – the operculum is close fitting – and can therefore withstand periods without moisture, for example at low tide or in the splash zone. They are all vegetarian. Although there is little interest in the group as a whole, one or two species are nonetheless collectors' favourites.

Nerita · Exuvia

Description

The body whorl has stout, rounded spiral ribs of dark grey, and between these it is a cream or pale beige, dotted with grey. The aperture wall is incised with grooves and is white, while the columella and parietal wall are granulose. This species lives in or near mangroves.

Other common names:
  Snake-skin Nerite
Author of the species, form or variety:
  L.
Date of publication:
  1758
Average size of mature shell:
  2.5 cm (1 in)
Locality:
  South-West Pacific
Habitat depth:
  Extends to about 25 m (83 ft)
Availability:
  Common

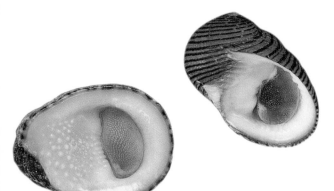

Nerita · Peloronta

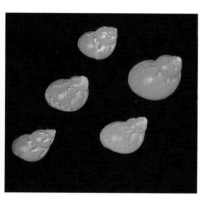

Description

Although very common, it is a popular species with its chracteristic blood-stained tooth pattern on the colummella and parietal area. The exterior can be either smooth or ridged and the colours vary. Most have a cream background, overlaid with spiral broken bands and dashes of red, lavender, grey and black. This nerite inhabits rocky shorelines.

Other common names:
    Bleeding Tooth Nerite
Author of the species, form or variety:
    L.
Date of publication:
    1758
Average size of mature shell:
    3 cm (1¼ in)
Locality:
    Caribbean
Habitat depth:
    Extends to about 25 m (83 ft)
Availability:
    Abundant

Nerita · Textilis

Description

Solid and chunky, this species has coarse, round spiral ribs, broken everywhere with fine axial growth lines. The colour is off-white, with broken grey patches on virtually every rib. The aperture is dentate and the parietal wall is pustulose. The operculum is a mid-grey and is also covered with tiny pustules. Found on shore rocks.

Other common names:
    Rough Nerite
Author of the species, form or variety:
    Gmelin
Date of publication:
    1791
Average size of mature shell:
    3 cm (1¼ in)
Locality:
    Indo-Pacific
Habitat depth:
    Extends to about 25 m (83 ft)
Availability:
    Common

Clypeolum · Latissimum

Description

A species with a most unusual shape, this is one of several in the subgenus *Clypeolum*.
It has a wide flaring mouth and a broad parietal shield. The exterior colouring is brown, grey or pale mauve, decorated with a fine black netted pattern. The aperture is grey and the columella and parietal area is a creamy yellow. The dark grey operculum is half-moon shaped. The species lives in estuaries and river mouths.

Other common names:
  Wide Nerite
Author of the species, form or variety:
  Broderip
Date of publication:
  1833
Average size of mature shell:
  3 cm (1¼ in)
Locality:
  Western Central America
Habitat depth:
  Extends to about 25 m (83 ft)
Availability:
  Common

Neritina · Communis

Description

Probably the most variably patterned of all gastropod species, its colours and patterns are virtually limitless! Most popular with collectors and shell lovers everywhere, this small shell is found among mangroves. It is smooth and glossy: the aperture being white or cream, tinged with pale orange, pink or red.

Other common names:
  Candy Nerite
Author of the species, form or variety:
  Quoy and Gaimard
Date of publication:
  1832
Average size of mature shell:
  1.5 cm (⅝ in)
Locality:
  Philippines
Habitat depth:
  Extends to about 25 m (83 ft)
Availability:
  Abundant

Smaragdia · Viridis

Description

A minute species, this probably the most popular of the very small nerites due to its vivid green colouring. It has a very low spire and a greatly enlarged body whorl. Two or three rows of white axial lines spiral agaubst the green background. The dentate columella extends to a large callous paietal shield in off-white. Emerald nerites live in shallow water.

Other common names:
  Emerald Nerite
Author of the species, form or variety:
  L.
Date of publication:
  1758
Average size of mature shell:
  6 mm (¼ in)
Locality:
  Caribbean
Habitat depth:
  Extends to about 25 m (83 ft)
Availability:
  Common

SUPER FAMILY
LITTORINOIDEA

FAMILY
LITTORINIDAE

The periwinkles are a group of
smallish shells numbering some 100
species – certain authorities suggest
fewer – some of which inhabit rocky
shores, while some are to be found in
mangroves. They are vegetarian and
feed on seaweed and algae. The group
is divided into several subfamilies,
such as *Littorininae* and *Tectariinae* (in
both of which we have an interest
here) and is further divided into many
genera. The family as a whole is not of
great interest to amateur collectors.

Littorina · Coccinea

Description

A relatively high spire and large angulate body whorl
distinguish this species, which is mostly smooth and
has no patterning. The colour can be white, beige or
lilac, and the aperture is presumably scarlet when
alive, the colour later fading to a pale orange.

Other common names:
  Scarlet Periwinkle
Author of the species, form or variety:
  Gmelin
Date of publication:
  1791
Average size of mature shell:
  2.5 cm (1 in)
Locality:
  Central and South-West Pacific
Habitat depth:
  Extends to about 25 m (83 ft)
Availability:
  Abundant

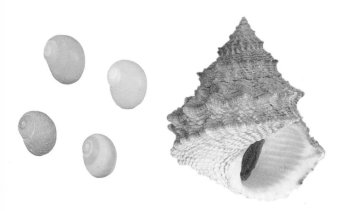

Littorina · Zebra

Tectarius · Coronatus

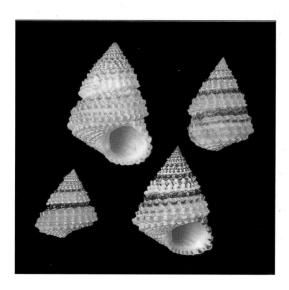

Description

A solid and low-spired shell, it is one of the most attractive in the genus, having a terracotta background with oblique brown stripes and tiny spiral grooves. The horny ovate operculum is dark brown in colour. This shell is found on intertidal rocks.

Description

A solid conical shell, it has spiral bands of coarse rounded nodules. The colours vary from overall cream or apricot to forms with strongly contrasting bands of orange and purple or pale and dark grey. They live on intertidal rocks.

Other common names:
  Striped Periwinkle
Author of the species, form or variety:
  Donovan
Date of publication:
  1825
Average size of mature shell:
  3 cm (1¼ in)
Locality:
  Costa Rica to Colombia
Habitat depth:
  Extends to about 25 m (83 ft)
Availability:
  Common

Other common names:
  Beaded Prickly Winkle
Author of the species, form or variety:
  Valenciennes
Date of publication:
  1832
Average size of mature shell:
  3 cm (1¼ in)
Locality:
  Philippines
Habitat depth:
  Extends to about 25 m (83 ft)
Availability:
  Abundant

SUPER FAMILY
CERITHIOIDEA

FAMILY
CERITHIIDAE
(Cerith Shells)

Most species of this major family are small. They are widely distributed in shallow, tropical seas, very few being found in European seas. All are vegetarian, living on diatoms and plant detritus, and they inhabit sand substrates, often in large colonies. They are generally long, tapering shells with many whorls, some with distinct sculpturing and patterns. In most species, the lower edge of the aperture develops an angled siphonal canal. The numerous genera include *Cerithium, Aluco* and *Rhinoclavis*.

Cerithium · Muscarum

Description

A small slender species, with coarse spiral nodules, it is middle-to-dark brown. The nodules, which in some shells are joined axially into ridges, are off-white. This is a shallow-water species – the two depicted were collected from Tarpoon Beach, Florida.

Other common names:
  Fly-specked Cerith
Author of the species, form or variety:
  Say
Date of publication:
  1832
Average size of mature shell:
  2.5 cm (1 in)
Locality:
  Southern Florida and West Indies
Habitat depth:
  Extends to about 25 m (83 ft)
Availability:
  Abundant

Cerithium · Muscarum

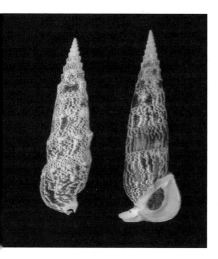

Pseudovertagus · Clava

Description

n markings and size this species is not unlike P. aluco, out is smoother with less prominent nodules on the whorls. The two depicted shells are both from Port Hedland, Western Australia. The shell is off-white, with mainly axial zigzag stripes and lines of dark grey or orown.

Description

One of the larger species in the family, its impressive shell is tall, with straight-sided whorls, the body whorl being rather flat at the anterior end. There are axial rows of low rounded nodules and incised spiral grooves. The colour is cream, with haphazard lines and patches of mid-brown. It lives in sand at depths to 40 m (132 ft).

Other common names:
Cumming's Cerith
Author of the species, form or variety:
A. Adams
Date of publication:
1855
Average size of mature shell:
8 cm (3¼ in)
Locality:
Western Australia
Habitat depth:
25 m (83 ft)
Availability:
Common

Other common names:
Club Vertagus
Author of the species, form or variety:
Gmelin
Date of publication:
1791
Average size of mature shell:
13 cm (5 in)
Locality:
Polynesia
Habitat depth:
Between 150 and 500 m
(495–1,650 ft)
Availability:
Rare

SUPER FAMILY
CERITHIOIDEA

FAMILY
CAMPANILIDAE
(Bell Clappers)

This was once a very large family of at least 700 species, all but one of which are known only from fossil remains. Many of these were found in the Paris Basin, France. One particular species grew to a length of at least 51 cm (20 in) – Campanile giganteum. The sole survivor, C. symbolicum is vegetarian and lives in a very restricted area in South-western Australia.

Campanile · Symbolicum

Description

There is only one genus in the Campanilidae family, and this, the only surviving species, is endemic to South-western Australia. The odd chalky white appearance gives it a fossil-like look. The spire is tall and has somewhat concave sides, the whorls bearing faint spiral grooves. There is no patterning. The glossy white columella is rather twisted.

Other common names:
Bell Clapper
Author of the species, form or variety:
Iredale
Date of publication:
1917
Average size of mature shell:
15 cm (6 in)
Locality:
South-western Australia
Habitat depth:
Extends to about 25 m (83 ft)
Availability:
Uncommon

SUPER FAMILY
CERITHIOIDEA

FAMILY
POTAMIDIDAE
(Horn Shells or Mud Creepers)

A group of shells of varying size, primarily brown in colour and more or less pointed and conical, they differ from the ceriths in that the outer lip of the aperture tends to be larger and expanded and the siphonal canal is short. They inhabit warm, muddy brackish waters in large groups and feed on marine detrital matter and algae. There are several genera, including Cerithidea, Telescopium and Terebralia.

Pyrazus · Ebeninus

Description

Dark brown to black, with fine spiral ridges, it has pronounced axially arranged nodules on a tall spire. The aperture is white on the columella but dark brown on the outer edge, and there is an upward fold at the posterior. These shells live in colonies on mud flats.

Other common names:
Ebony Mud Creeper
Author of the species, form or variety:
Bruguière
Date of publication:
1792
Average size of mature shell:
10 cm (4 in)
Locality:
Eastern Australia
Habitat depth:
Extends to about 25 m (83 ft)
Availability:
Abundant

Tympanotonus · Fuscatus

Description

This beautifully ornamented shell has a tall, slender spire. Rows of small rounded spiral tubercules and most prominent sharp and slightly upturned nodules characterize this species. The variety *T. fuscatus radula* lacks the sharp nodules, but is covered with spiral tuberculose beading. The spires are usually partly eroded. Both forms are shown here, and both samples come from Sazaire, Angola.

Other common names:
  West African Mud Creeper
Author of the species, form or variety:
  L.
Date of publication:
  1758
Average size of mature shell:
  5.5 cm (2¼ in)
Locality:
  Central West Africa
Habitat depth:
  Extends to about 25 m (83 ft)
Availability:
  Common

Tympanotonus · Palustris

Description

A large species, with flat axial ribs and rows of spiral grooves, the mud creeper has a flaring aperture which is shiny inside, with black spiral striae. The columella is creamy white. The outer colour is mid-brown. This is another mangrove mud-flat dweller.

Other common names:
  Mud Creeper
Author of the species, form or variety:
  L.
Date of publication:
  1767
Average size of mature shell:
  12 cm (4 ¾ in)
Locality:
  Indo-Pacific
Habitat depth:
  25 m (83 ft)
Availability:
  Common

SUPER FAMILY
CERITHIOIDEA

FAMILY
TURRITELLIDAE
(Screw Shells)

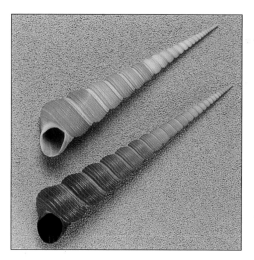

Two main genera within this family concern us here – Turritella and Vermicularia. The former genus are the true screw shells and have very tall spires and regular tightly coiled whorls, whereas the latter begin with several regular whorls and then suddenly grow in a haphazard and quite unruly direction. Neither type possesses a siphonal canal. There are over 100 species, all of which are vegetarian, and inhabit offshore waters in coarse sand or mud. This is not a particularly popular family with collectors.

Turritella · Terebra

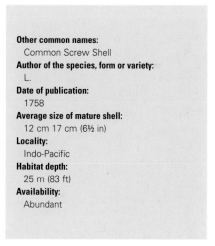

Description

A large species, with flat axial ribs and rows of spiral grooves, the mud creeper has a flaring aperture which is shiny inside, with black spiral striae. The columella is creamy white. The outer colour is mid-brown. This is another mangrove mud-flat dweller.

Other common names:
  Common Screw Shell
Author of the species, form or variety:
  L.
Date of publication:
  1758
Average size of mature shell:
  12 cm 17 cm (6½ in)
Locality:
  Indo-Pacific
Habitat depth:
  25 m (83 ft)
Availability:
  Abundant

Turritella · Cingulata

Description

A short solid species, it is cream in colour, with several rows of broad dark brown spiral bands. The whorls are generally straight sided and number between eight and ten. It lives in subtidal waters.

Other common names:
  Banded Screw Shell
Author of the species, form or variety:
  Sowerby
Date of publication:
  1825
Average size of mature shell:
  7.5 cm (3 in)
Locality:
  Chile
Habitat depth:
  Extends to about 25 m (83 ft)
Availability:
  Common

Turritella · Radula

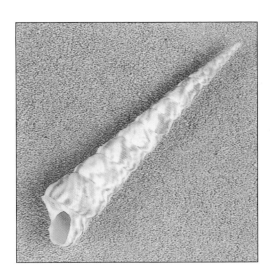

Description

A short solid species, it is cream in colour, with several rows of broad dark brown spiral bands. The whorls are generally straight sided and number between eight and ten. It lives in subtidal waters.

Other common names:
  Dart Turritella
Author of the species, form or variety:
  Kiener
Date of publication:
  1843
Average size of mature shell:
  10 cm (4 in)
Locality:
  Gulf of California to Mexico
Habitat depth:
  25 m (83 ft)
Availability:
  Uncommon

Turritella · Ungulina

Description

A robust species, its well rounded whorls – about 14 on mature specimens – bear fine spiral ribs. The colour varies from pure white through to a near black, most being middle-to-dark brown. This shell is often used in local native jewellery.

Other common names:
  Rounded Screw Shell
Author of the species, form or variety:
  L.
Date of publication:
  1758
Average size of mature shell:
  8 cm (3¼ in)
Locality:
  West Africa
Habitat depth:
  Extends to about 25 m (83 ft)
Availability:
  Common

Vermicularia · Spirata

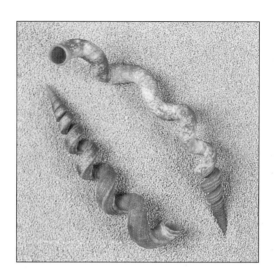

Description

For obvious reasons, the common name is very apt. The shell in its early growth period starts very much like other turritellas, but after about six whorls the growth becomes open and haphazard. There are two or three spiral ribs which are not evident nearer the aperture. The shells live among sponges in shallow water.

Other common names:
  Caribbean Worm Shell
Author of the species, form or variety:
  Philippi
Date of publication:
  1836
Average size of mature shell:
  11.5 cm (4½ in)
Locality:
  Southern Florida and Caribbean Sea
Habitat depth:
  Extends to about 25 m (83 ft)
Availability:
  Common

SUPER FAMILY
CERITHIOIDEA

FAMILY
SILIQUARIIDAE
(Worm Shells)

Although previously placed with the genus Vermicularia, these worm shells are now within a family of their own. They differ from the former group in that they produce virtually no spire, but a kind of tubular chamber. The early whorls are often flat or depressed and, where these two grow in a haphazard manner, there is a distinct slit or opening running along the entire length of the shell, except at the apex. They often live in colonies on substrate.

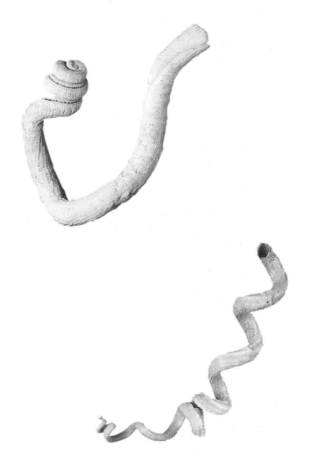

Siliquaria · Ponderosa

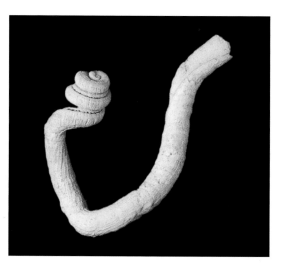

Description

This bizarre species is a popular collectors' item. Large flatly-coiled early whorls grow out into strange haphazard forms, taking no set shape. The sculpturing is scaly and off-white, with many growth lines and scars. The open slit is more evident on the earlier growth, becoming somewhat covered with age. This specimen was fished off Taiwan.

Other common names:
  Giant Worm Shell
Author of the species, form or variety:
  Mörch
Date of publication:
  1860
Average size of mature shell:
  30 cm (12 in)
Locality:
  Taiwan and Indo-Pacific
Habitat depth:
  Extends to about 25 m (83 ft)
Availability:
  Uncommon

Siliquaria · Cumingi

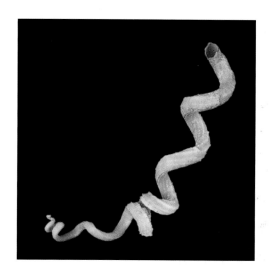

Description

Another greatly distorted species, it is finer than S. ponderosa, and has several spiral ribs on which are small scaly projections. The slit is evident through the entire length of the shell. The dirty pink or beige surface is often lime-encrusted.

Other common names:
  Scaled Worm Shell
Author of the species, form or variety:
  Mörch
Date of publication:
  1860
Average size of mature shell:
  20 cm (8 in)
Locality:
  Taiwan to Philippines
Habitat depth:
  Extends to about 25 m (83 ft)
Availability:
  Uncommon

SUPER FAMILY
STROMBOIDEA

FAMILY
APORRHAIDAE
(Pelican's Foot Shells)

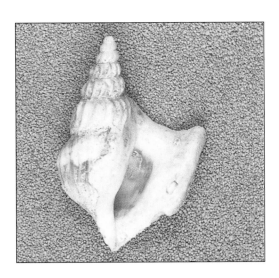

A small family of about six species, the pelican's foot shells occur in the cooler waters of the North Atlantic and Mediterranean. The outer lip bears characteristic finger-like processes from which the common name derives. Many strangely-shaped fossil species are known. The living species are fairly mobile and are mainly sand dwellers.

Aporrhais · Occidentalis

Description

The thickest and heaviest of the group, this shell inhabits deep water to about 600 m (1,980 ft). It is usually heavily encrusted or eroded but some ornamentation – coarse axial ribs and fine spiral lirae – can be seen. The thickened outer lip does not bear projections as in the other aporrhais. This specimen was dredged off Maine, USA.

Other common names:
American Pelican's Foot
Author of the species, form or variety:
Beck
Date of publication:
1836
Average size of mature shell:
5 cm (2 in)
Locality:
Eastern Canada to North Carolina
Habitat depth:
Between 150 and 500 m (495–1,650 ft)
Availability:
Uncommon

Aporrhais · Pespelicani

Aporrhais ·Senegalensis

Description

Coarsely sculptured, with angled and nodulose whorls, its extended and thickened lip bears four projections – one growing alongside the spire, two growing outwards and the fourth forming the siphonal canal. The colour is generally cream or off-white. The aperture, columella, and interior of the processes are often calloused and glazed. It inhabits relatively deep water, to about 175 m (575 ft).

Description

This is the smallest member of the family. It has a medium-sized spire and each whorl bears spiral rounded nodules. It has three projections and a narrow siphonal canal. The shell is beige brown. The specimen seen here came from Gabon.

Other common names:
  Common Pelican's Foot
Author of the species, form or variety:
  L.
Date of publication:
  1758
Average size of mature shell:
  4 cm (1½ in)
Locality:
  Mediterranean to Norway
Habitat depth:
  Between 150 and 500 m (495–1,650 ft)
Availability:
  Common

Other common names:
  Senegalese Pelican's Foot
Author of the species, form or variety:
  Gray
Date of publication:
  1838
Average size of mature shell:
  2.5 cm (1 in)
Locality:
  West Africa
Habitat depth:
  Between 25 and 150 m (83-495 ft)
Availability:
  Uncommon

SUPER FAMILY
STROMBOIDEA

FAMILY
STROMBIDAE
(Conch Shells)

This is a large, well-known and diverse family. Strombus possess what is known as the stromboid notch – an indentation at the anterior end of the aperture through which the animal can protrude its stalked eye. The operculum is seldom large enough to close the aperture but is often used as an aid to mobility or as a defensive weapon against predatory crustaceans and fish. The Lambis all have flaring lips with long digit-like projections, siphonal canal and a pronounced stromboid notch. The Tibia species, however, are generally fusiform, with extended canals, curved anal canals, and tall multi-whorled spires. The species of Varicospira discussed are not unlike Tibia species, but with short canals, while Terebellum bear little resemblance to the true conches. All species are vegetarian.

Lambis · Wheelwrighti

Description

Some of the most interesting and distinctive-looking large marine gastropods are the members of the genus Lambis found exclusively in the Indo-Pacific region, its species readily exhibit traits not so easily recognizable in other families. One such trait is sexual dimorphism of shells. The digits are short, and there are rounded nodules on the whorls. The aperture is a pale pinkish orange, with darker streaked lirae inside. The columella and spire are calloused.

Other common names:
    Wheelwright's Spider Conch
Author of the species, form or variety:
    Greene
Date of publication:
    1978
Average size of mature shell:
    20 cm (8 in)
Locality:
    Philippines
Habitat depth:
    Extends to about 25 m (83 ft)
Availability:
    Uncommon

Lambis · Chiragra arthritica

Description

Resembling *L. chiragra chiragra*, but much smaller, the body whorl of this shell is rather bulbous and bears very strong rounded ribs. The hollow digits are relatively short and curved, and the columella and parietal area is strongly lirate. There is dark brown or purple staining around the aperture of the mottled brown shell. It inhabits coral reefs.

Other common names:
    Arthritic Spider Conch
Author of the species, form or variety:
    Röding
Date of publication:
    1798
Average size of mature shell:
    15 cm (6 in)
Locality:
    East Africa
Habitat depth:
    Extends to about 25 m (83 ft)
Availability:
    Common

Strombus · Latissimus

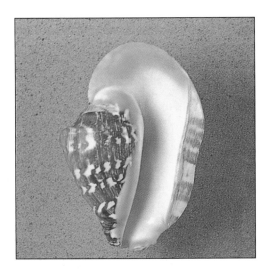

Description

The solid and very heavy shell has a wide flaring lip, which is much thickened at the margins, opposite the columella. The spire is low and partly obscured by the posterior part of the lip. Shells are generally encrusted with marine deposits, but when clean they are a pale or middle shade of brown, with axial lines and blotches which become darker and more vivid on the underside of the body whorl. The aperture is white. The shell seen here is from the Central Philippines.

Other common names:
  Wide-mouthed Conch
Author of the species, form or variety:
  L.
Date of publication:
  1758
Average size of mature shell:
  15 cm (6 in)
Locality:
  West Pacific
Habitat depth:
  Extends to about 25 m (83 ft)
Availability:
  Common

Strombus · Sinuatus

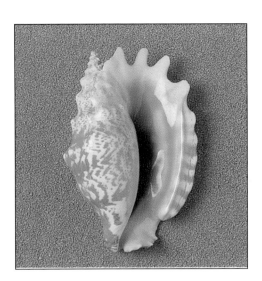

Description

This is a lovely shell, with attractive colouring, a moderate spire and a long convex body whorl. The outer lip, thickened opposite the columella, extends at the posterior with four or so short rounded tab-like projections. The shell is off-white, with russet axial striations and blotches. The aperture is pale pink, with deep purple staining. The specimen shown here was collected on coarse coral sand in shallow water, Central Philippines.

Other common names:
  Laciniate Conch
Author of the species, form or variety:
  Lightfoot
Date of publication:
  1786
Average size of mature shell:
  10 cm (4 in)
Locality:
  South-West Pacific
Habitat depth:
  Extends to about 25 m (83 ft)
Availability:
  Common

Strombus · Granulatus

Strombus · Tricornis

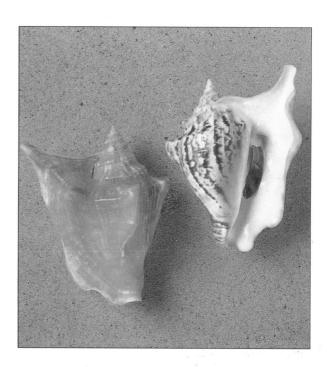

Description

The granulated conch is rather tall and slender with strong tubercules and rough spiral ribs. It features broad bands of brown on white. The aperture is white, and fine granulations occur on the inside of the lip in mature specimens. The margins are tinged with creamy yellow, as is the parietal wall. This specimen is from Gubernadora Island, Panama.

Description

Although there are many rounded nodules on the shoulders, there are usually two or three which are larger, and it is from these that the common name is derived. A smaller conch, it has a wide lip that extends into a finger-like projection at the posterior. Colours and patterns vary greatly. It is found in shallow water on sand and is endemic.

Other common names:
  Granulated Conch
Author of the species, form or variety:
  Swainson
Date of publication:
  1822
Average size of mature shell:
  7.5 cm (3 in)
Locality:
  Western Central America
Habitat depth:
  25 m (83 ft)
Availability:
  Common

Other common names:
  Three-knobbed Conch
Author of the species, form or variety:
  Lightfoot
Date of publication:
  1786
Average size of mature shell:
  10 cm (4 in)
Locality:
  Red Sea and Gulf of Aden
Habitat depth:
  Extends to about 25 m (83 ft)
Availability:
  Common

Strombus · Epidromis

Description

A bulbous rounded shell, its moderate spire is formed of angular whorls which are smooth in texture, although early whorls bear minute spiral striae and axial ribs. The shell is off-white, overlaid with a fine pale brown 'netting' pattern. The aperture is pure white and highly glossy. A shallow-water dweller, it is found in mud or sand.

Other common names:
  Swan Conch
Author of the species, form or variety:
  L.
Date of publication:
  1758
Average size of mature shell:
  7.5 cm (3 in)
Locality:
  South-West Pacific
Habitat depth:
  Extends to about 25 m (83 ft)
Availability:
  Common

Terebellum · Terebellum

Description

These slim, highly glossy and smooth shells bear little resemblance to true conches. They are bullet-shaped and slightly convex, with short spires and an enlarged body whorl which is truncated at the anterior end. The patterns are highly variable – several forms are shown here. They inhabit subtidal sandy areas.

Other common names:
  Little Auger Shell
Author of the species, form or variety:
  L.
Date of publication:
  1758
Average size of mature shell:
  4 cm (1½ in)
Locality:
  Indo-Pacific
Habitat depth:
  Between 25 and 150 m (83–495 ft)
Availability:
  Common

Tibia · Delicatula

Description

The delicate tibia is rather like a miniature *T. insulaechorab*, but with quite a different aperture. The canal is very short and slightly curved and there are about four short projections on the lip margin. The posterior canal is virtually non-existent. It is pale beige overall, with four cream spiral bands on the body whorl. The aperture is pale creamy white. This is a deep-water species.

Other common names:
: Delicate Tibia
Author of the species, form or variety:
Nevill
Date of publication:
1881
Average size of mature shell:
7.5 cm (3 in)
Locality:
Indian Ocean
Habitat depth:
Between 150-500 m (495 and 1,650 ft)
Availability:
Common

Tibia · Insulaechorab

Description

A solid, thick, and heavy shell, with a high spire, the Arabian tibia has gently rounded whorls and its body whorl is wide and bulbous. It has minute axial ribs near the apex and faint growth striae throughout. The siphonal canal is very short and slightly curved; the posterior canal of the sample shown here has grown against the spire for about 2.5 cm (1 in) and is heavily calloused. The overall colour is mid-brown and glossy, and there is a white aperture and columella. The lip margin bears six or seven stunted denticles.

Other common names:
Arabian Tibia
Author of the species, form or variety:
Röding
Date of publication:
1798
Average size of mature shell:
14 cm (5½in)
Locality:
Indian Ocean
Habitat depth:
Extends to about 25 m (83 ft) and between 25 and 150 m (83–495 ft)
Availability:
Common

Tibia · Martini

Description

This generally thin and lightweight shell has rounded whorls and a fairly short straight siphonal canal. There are four or five very stunted denticles on the lip margin. A one-time rarity, it has now become readily available, due to deep-sea commercial fishing in the late 1960s.

Other common names:
  Martin's Tibia
Author of the species, form or variety:
  Marratt
Date of publication:
  1877
Average size of mature shell:
  12 cm (4¾ in)
Locality:
  Philippines
Habitat depth:
  Between 150 and 500 m
  (495–1,650 ft)
Availability:
  Common

Varicospira · Cancellata

Description

A small ovate shell, it has a moderate spire and rounded whorls. Fine spiral lirae are evident, as well as strong rounded axial ribs, these two features giving the shell its cancellate texture. The aperture is white; the siphonal canal short; and the anterior canal extends at least half-way up the side of the spire. This shell is found in offshore waters.

Other common names:
  Cancellate Tibia
Author of the species, form or variety:
  Lamarck
Date of publication:
  1822
Average size of mature shell:
  3 cm (1¼ in)
Locality:
  Indo-Pacific
Habitat depth:
  Between 150 and 500 m
  (495–1,650 ft)
Availability:
  Uncommon

SUPER FAMILY
CREPIDULOIDEA

FAMILY
CREPIDULIDAE
(Slipper, Cup, and Saucer Shells)

Crepidula · Maculosa

A relatively small group of gastropods, these are either rock dwellers or live on the backs of other shelled creatures. All possess either a shelf-like or a cup-shaped structure in order to protect the soft organs. They are generally flat, rounded or slipper-shaped and can be smooth, ridged or spiny. They are distributed globally, filter-feeding on vegetable matter. There are several genera and subgenera, notably Crepidula, Calyptraea, Trochita and Crucibulum.

Description

A small flat ovate species, it invariably lives on the backs of other shells. Colours and patterns vary, a selection being shown here. The small shelflife structure occupies a third to the half of the interior cavity. It is an inhabitant of subtidal waters, these examples coming from Yucatán Mexico.

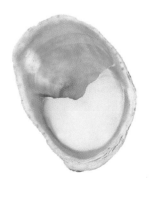

Other common names:
   Spotted Slipper Limpet
Author of the species, form or variety:
   Conrad
Date of publication:
   1846
Average size of mature shell:
   2.5 cm (1 in)
Locality:
   Gulf of Mexico and Bahamas
Habitat depth:
   Between 25 and 150 m (83-495 ft)
Availability:
   Common

Tibia · Martini

Description

This generally thin and lightweight shell has rounded whorls and a fairly short straight siphonal canal. There are four or five very stunted denticles on the lip margin. A one-time rarity, it has now become readily available, due to deep-sea commercial fishing in the late 1960s.

Other common names:
   Martin's Tibia
Author of the species, form or variety:
   Marratt
Date of publication:
   1877
Average size of mature shell:
   12 cm (4¾ in)
Locality:
   Philippines
Habitat depth:
   Between 150 and 500 m
   (495–1,650 ft)
Availability:
   Common

Trochita · Trochiformis

Description

A rounded flattish shell, it is often heavily encrusted with marine debris. The dorsum, where obvious, is ridged. The underside is similar to trochus shells; the 'shelf hair' area occupies at least half of the shell. An inhabitant of offshore rocks, this specimen is from Iquiquie, Chile.

Other common names:
   Peruvian Hat
Author of the species, form, or variety:
   Born
Date of publication:
   1778
Average size of mature shell:
   5.5 cm (2¼ in)
Locality:
   Western South America
Habitat depth:
   Between 25 and 150 m (83–495 ft)
Availability:
   Common

SUPER FAMILY
XENOPHOROIDEA

FAMILY
XENOPHORIDAE
(Carrier Shells)

One of the most fascinating families in the phylum Mollusca, these are truly the 'original shell collectors!' The group is fairly small, with a single genus – Xenophora – which contains several subgenera, including Stellaria, Tugurium and Onustus. They are all basically trochoidal in shape, with flattish bases. The animal uses its foot to gather dead shells, pebbles, coral and marine debris and uses a secretion to cement these objects to its own shell. A few species of Xenophora do not collect material; nor do Stellaria species. There are several theories as to why this group covers itself with marine objects: camouflage against predators; to add strength and rigidity to a fragile shell; and to stop the carrier shell from sinking into muddy substrate. Measurements given are for mature shells without attachments.

Tugurium · Giganteum

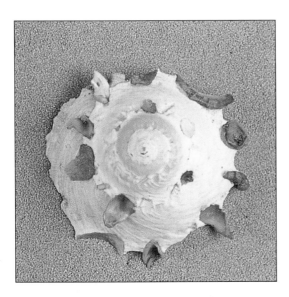

Description

This large thin shell has flat sides and a broad base. Small shell fragments are attached along the suture and at the periphery of the body whorl. There are very fine axial growth striae and very fine radial striae on the underside. It is a pale beige or white colour. This specimen was dredged at 300 m (990 ft) off Natal, South Africa.

Other common names:
  Great Carrier Shell
Author of the species, form, or variety:
  Schepman
Date of publication:
  1909
Average size of mature shell:
  10 cm (4 in)
Locality:
  South Africa and Japan
Habitat depth:
  Between 150 and 500 m (495–1,650 ft)
Availability:
  Uncommon

Xenophora • Crispa

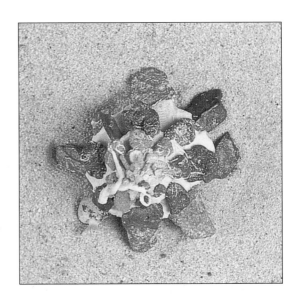

Description

This small but solid conical shell has fine spiral lirae. These also occur on the underside, radiating from a part-open umbilicus. The creature collects smooth and rough pebbles. This shell was trawled at 65 m (215 ft) off Malaga, Spain.

Other common names:
  Mediterranean Carrier Shell
Author of the species, form, or variety:
  Koenig
Date of publication:
  1831
Average size of mature shell:
  3 cm (1¼ in)
Locality:
  Mediterranean and North-East Atlantic
Habitat depth:
  Between 150 and 500 m (495–1,650 ft)
Availability:
  Common

SUPER FAMILY
CYPRAEOIDEA

FAMILY
CYPRAEIDAE
(Cowrie Shells)

Among collectors, this is probably the most popular family of molluscs, possibly due to their very smooth, glossy porcelain-like texture and vivid patterning and colouration. It is a large group, in excess of 200 named species, with many varieties and local variations, and the number is constantly being augmented. There is one main genus, Cypraea, which over the years has been divided into many and various subgenera, taking into account differences of anatomy as well as shell structure. Kay Vaught lists 55 subgenera. However, for simplicity's sake this book will adhere to Cypraea throughout, although mention will be made of subgeneric names where necessary. The listed specimens are arranged approximately according to their global distribution.

Cypraea · Cinerea

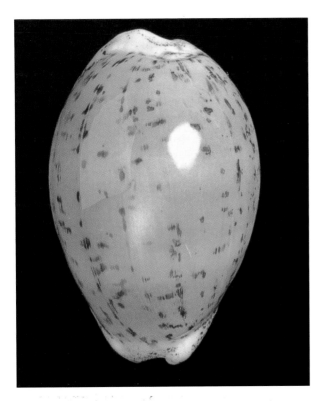

Cypraea · Zebra

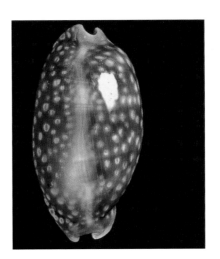

Description

A sturdy little shell, with a rather humped dorsum and convex base, it has fine grooved teeth at either side of a curved aperture. The colour is a pinky grey, overlaid with black dots and blotches, more so at the margins, which are slightly inflated on mature specimens. This shell inhabits rocky reefs in shallow water.

Description

Sometimes confused with small *C. cervus*, this can be distinguished by its more slender, less inflated shape and more importantly by the occurrence of ocellated spots on the lateral margins. It is dark brown with grey spots and fairly coarse, almost black, teeth, especially on the outer lip. It swells in shallow water.

Other common names:
  Atlantic Gray Cowrie
Author of the species, form, or variety:
  Gmelin
Date of publication:
  1791
Average size of mature shell:
  3 cm (1¼ in)
Locality:
  South-eastern USA to Brazil
Habitat depth:
  Extends to about 25 m (83 ft)
Availability:
  Common

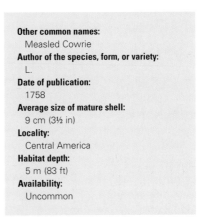

Other common names:
  Measled Cowrie
Author of the species, form, or variety:
  L.
Date of publication:
  1758
Average size of mature shell:
  9 cm (3½ in)
Locality:
  Central America
Habitat depth:
  5 m (83 ft)
Availability:
  Uncommon

Cypraea · Capensis

Cypraea · Cervus

Description

Until recent scuba diving activity, South African cowries were rarely found alive. In this species, coarse ribs spiral around the entire shell, thinning at the columella lip and thickening at the labial lip. There is a distinct, dark brown blotch on the dorsum. Its range extends from shallow to moderately deep water.

Description

Although the largest species of the genus, it is rare nowadays to find specimens over about 15 cm (6 in). The shell is large, ovate and rather inflated but lightweight. It is mid-brown in colour, with pale grey dots which cease at the margins. There is a wide dorsal line. The prominent teeth are dark brown and more numerous on the columella lip. The interior is pale lavender.

Other common names:
Cape Cowrie
Author of the species, form, or variety:
Grey
Date of publication:
1828
Average size of mature shell:
3 cm (1½ in)
Locality:
South Africa
Habitat depth:
Between 25 m (83 ft)
Availability:
Uncommon

Other common names:
Atlantic Deer Cowrie
Author of the species, form, or variety:
L.
Date of publication:
1771
Average size of mature shell:
19 cm (7½ in)
Locality:
Florida and Caribbean
Habitat depth:
Extends to about 25 m (83 ft)
Availability:
Uncommon

Cypraea · Onyx

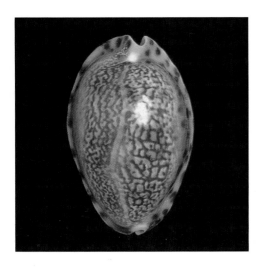

Description

The humped dorsum, ovate shape and sharply defined margins provide the identification points of this little shell. The dorsal colour is pale green, overlaid with brown reticulation; the margins are pale grey with strong black spots. The flattish base is a pinkish beige, and the teeth are fine. It lives under rocks and slabs at low tide levels.

Other common names:
  Little Arabian Cowrie
Author of the species, form, or variety:
  Lamarck
Date of publication:
  1810
Average size of mature shell:
  3 cm (1¼ in)
Locality:
  Western Central America
Habitat depth:
  25 m (83 ft)
Availability:
  Common

Cypraea · Onyx

Description

A variation of *C. onyx*, it is one of several variations within this little group. The shell is pyriform, and is moderately humped, with a convex base. It is a handsome variety, being a rich brown, almost black, with reddish brown teeth which are short but strong. Some young examples display broad spiral banding.

Other common names:
  F. adusta. Dark Onyx Cowrie
Author of the species, form, or variety:
  Lamarck
Date of publication:
  1810
Average size of mature shell:
  5 cm (2 in)
Locality:
  East Africa
Habitat depth:
  Extends to about 25 m (83 ft)
Availability:
  Common

Cypraea · Aurantium

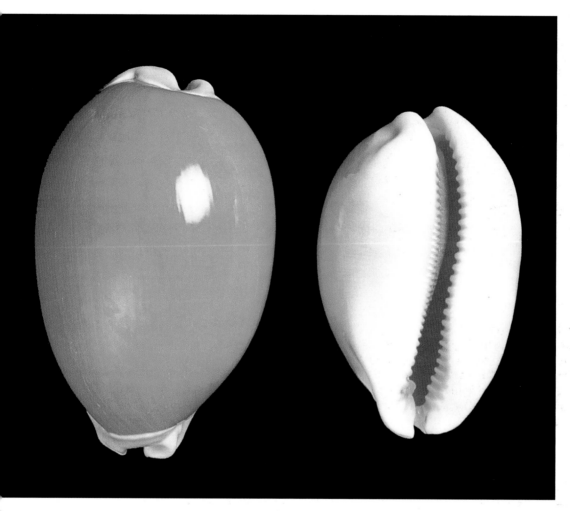

Description

Highly prized among collectors, the purchase price is usually totally out of proportion to its rarity; indeed they are relatively common shells in Samar Island, Philippines, where they inhabit rocky ledges and holes at depths of about 20 m (65 ft). However, demand exceeds supply. The large, ovate and inflated shell is not 'golden' in fact, but a deep magenta when fresh, fading to a deep orange. The base is pinkish beige and the teeth are tinged with orange.

Other common names:
Golden Cowrie
Author of the species, form, or variety:
Gmelin
Date of publication:
1791
Average size of mature shell:
10 cm (4 in)
Locality:
Philippines, Solomon Islands and Fiji
Habitat depth:
Between 25 and 150 m (83–495 ft)
Availability:
Rare

Cypraea · Cribraria

Description

A very strikingly marked shell, it occurs in many forms and locality variations. This species is pure white, both above and below, and the dorsum is overlaid with a rich ochre and brown network, producing stark large white circular spots. It is probably the most common of all the **cribraria** varieties.

Other common names:
  Sieve Cowrie
Author of the species, form, or variety:
  L.
Date of publication:
  1758
Average size of mature shell:
  4 cm (1½ in)
Locality:
  Indo-Pacific
Habitat depth:
  Extends to about 25 m (83 ft)
Availability:
  Common

Cypraea · Caputdraconis

Description

This endemic ovate-to-rounded shell has a moderately humped dorsum. The teeth are short and coarse, and the base is flat. It is dark brown overall, with small dorsal spots and blotches of white. The posterior and anterior canal areas are coloured a pale blue grey, and the base is a paler grey brown, with off-white teeth. It inhabits shallow rough water, living under rocks and coral.

Other common names:
  Dragon Head Cowrie
Author of the species, form, or variety:
  Melvill
Date of publication:
  1888
Average size of mature shell:
  4 cm (1½ in)
Locality:
  Easter Island
Habitat depth:
  Extends to about 25 m (83 ft)
Availability:
  Common

Cypraea · Rosselli

Cypraea · Argus

Description

A well-known and widespread species, it is characteristically cylindrical and elongated. There are brown stained, moderately coarse teeth; three dark brown basal blotches and one which is less dark; and the dorsum is covered with irregular rings or 'eyes' and odd blotches of dark brown over a beige ground colour. Another unmistakable shell.

Description

Probably the rarest of the subgenus *Zoila,* to which *C. friendii* and *C. marginarta* also belong. It is almost deltoid in shape, with a steeply humped dorsum, and is a very rich dark brown to black, usually with a creamy white and irregularly patched dorsum. A moderately deep-water species, it is collected in crayfish pots or by scuba divers.

Other common names:
 Eyed Cowrie
Author of the species, form, or variety:
 L.
Date of publication:
 1758
Average size of mature shell:
 7.5 cm (3 in)
Locality:
 Indo-Pacific
Habitat depth:
 Extends to about 25 m (83 ft)
Availability:
 Common

Other common names:
 Rossell's Cowrie
Author of the species, form, or variety:
 Cotton
Date of publication:
 1948
Average size of mature shell:
 5 cm (2 in)
Locality:
 South-western Australia
Habitat depth:
 Between 25 and 150 m (83–495 ft)
Availability:
 Rare

SUPER FAMILY
CYPRAEOIDEA

FAMILY
OVULIDAE
(Egg Shells)

Closely related to and not dissimilar from true cowries. Cypraeidae, the egg shells or false cowries are a family of species which are generally pyriform or spindle-shaped, with few or no teeth. There are some anatomical differences between these and true cowries, and egg shells lack patterning or markings. Most inhabit tropical seas, mainly in the Indo-Pacific areas, where they live in close proximity to sponges, sea fans and soft corals and gorgonians. There are several well-known genera, such as Jennaria, Ovula, Calpurnus, Cyphoma, Phenacovolva, Primovula and Volva, each differing in characteristic shape or form. They are therefore varied enough to promote more than a cursory interest among collectors.

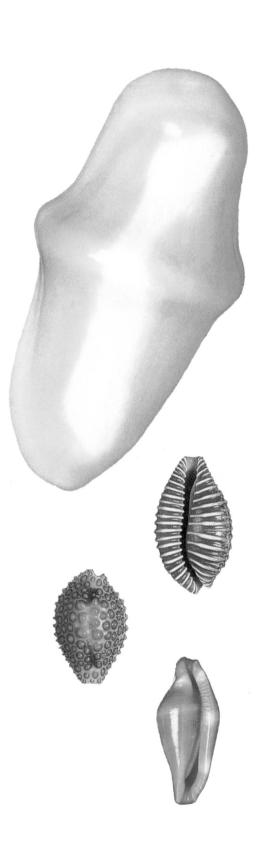

Calpurnus · Verrucosus

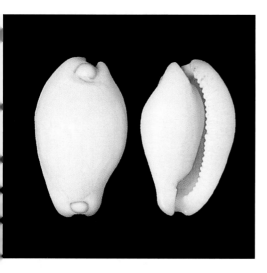

Description

A strange species, the warted egg shell has a raised rounded tubercule just above the posterior and anterior canals. It is ovate, with a raised spiral ridge on the dorsum. The lip bears coarse teeth. The extremities are tinged with pink. This shell inhabits shallow-water reef areas.

Other common names:
  Warted Egg Shell
Author of the species, form, or variety:
  L.
Date of publication:
  1758
Average size of mature shell:
  3 cm (1¼ in)
Locality:
  Indo-Pacific
Habitat depth:
  Extends to about 25 m (83 ft)
Availability:
  Common

Hiatavolva · Depressa

Description

A delicate long narrow shell, it widens slightly at the centre and has shortened truncated canals. The lip is thick and the aperture is very narrow, widening at the anterior. In colour it is pale pink or yellow, the extremities being tinged with crimson.

Other common names:
  Depressed Volva
Author of the species, form, or variety:
  Sowerby
Date of publication:
  1875
Average size of mature shell:
  3 cm (1¼ in)
Locality:
  Western Australia
Habitat depth:
  25 m (83 ft)
Availability:
  Uncommon

Ovula · Ovum

Description

A well-known shell, it is very similar to *O. costellata,* but much larger, inflated and not at all angular. There is no spire, and the lip is coarsely ridged on the underside. The anterior canal is pronounced. The outer shell is a glossy white throughout and the interior is a deep orange brown. A shallow-water reef dweller.

Other common names:
    Common Egg Shell
Author of the species, form, or variety:
    L.
Date of publication:
    1758
Average size of mature shell:
    9 cm (3½ in)
Locality:
    Indo-Pacific
Habitat depth:
    Extends to about 25 m (83 ft)
Availability:
    Common

Ovula · Ovum

Description

This lightweight shell is ovate, with extended extremities and a moderately humped dorsum. It is very pale pink or cream , the underside being a pale yellow, and there is a faint deep pink tint along the inner edge of the lip. This specimen was dredged in shrimp nets off Vitória, Espírito Santo, Brazil.

Other common names:
    Intermediate Cyphoma
Author of the species, form, or variety:
    Sowerby
Date of publication:
    1828
Average size of mature shell:
    4 cm (1½ in)
Locality:
    Caribbean to Brazil
Habitat depth:
    Between 25 and 150 m (83-495 ft)
Availability:
    Rare

Gastropoda 85

Volva · Volva

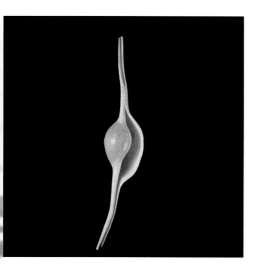

Description

One of the most amazing shells, this has an extraordinary shape: the body whorl is ovate and globose, with fine spiral grooves, the lip being slightly thickened, and the canals extremely long, narrow and obliquely ridged. Overall, it is a pale cream-to-pink, with very slightly darker extremities. A collectors' favourite, it can be found on or near coral reefs.

Other common names:
Shuttle Shell
Author of the species, form, or variety:
L.
Date of publication:
1758
Average size of mature shell:
17 cm (6½ in)
Locality:
Indo-Pacific
Habitat depth:
Extends to about 25 m (83 ft)
Availability:
Common

SUPER FAMILY
CYPRAEOIDEA

FAMILY
TRIVIIDAE
(Allied Cowries)

A small group, they are often termed true cowries, but this can be misleading. Although in many respects the Triviidae resemble Cypraea, there are anatomical differences and the former have prominent ridges and are generally less glossy.

Trivia · Monacha

Description

A tiny solid rounded shell, it has a high dorsum and is encircled with tiny ribs. The lip is thickened and rounded. The colour is a pale grey, sometimes pinkish, with three prominent dorsal spots of a grey brown. The base is white. These two specimens were collected on the Portuguese coast.

Other common names:
European or Bean Cowrie
Author of the species, form, or variety:
Da Costa
Date of publication:
1778
Average size of mature shell:
1 cm (⅜ in)
Locality:
North-East Atlantic and Mediterranean
Habitat depth:
Extends to about 25 m (83 ft)
Availability:
Common

SUPER FAMILY
NATICOIDEA

FAMILY
NATICIDAE
(Moon or Necklace Shells)

A large worldwide family of smooth, glossy shells with depressed spires and enlarged body whorls, they are all carnivorous, feeding on other molluscs and similar creatures, and living in sand. The group is split into subfamilies, separated by differences in the form of the operculum. There are numerous genera and subgenera, notably Globularia, Polinices, Natica, Sinum, Lunatia and Stigmaulax. Valuable contributions to the study of Naticidae have been made by Mike Dixon (UK) and Marc Streitz (France), both amateur enthusiasts. Professionals Cernorsky, Kilburn and Marincovich have written on the Naticas of certain areas, but a full pictorial guide is still lacking.

Euspira · Lewisi

Description

The largest species in the family Naticidae, Lewis' moon is thick and heavy, often scarred or encrusted, and is a chalky beige white, with numerous growth striae. The interior is pale brown, as are the outer edges of the lip, columella and calloused parietal wall. There is an open umbilicus. A popular collectors' shell, it lives in sand. The depicted specimen is from the Puget Sound, Washington, USA.

Other common names:
  Lewis's Moon
Author of the species, form, or variety:
  Gould
Date of publication:
  1847
Average size of mature shell:
  10 cm (4 in)
Locality:
  Western USA
Habitat depth:
  Extends to about 25 m (83 ft)
Availability:
  Common

Polinices · Grossularia

Natica · Stellata

Description

This bright orange glossy shell is very attractive. There are spiral patches of white and yellow. The interior, columella and parietal wall are pure white. The umbilicus is deep, although partly covered by the calloused parietal area. This is another shallow-water sand dweller.

Description

A lightweight fragile species, it has a large rounded body whorl and a distinct umbilicus. The operculum is thin and horny. The shell is a pale beige overlaid with spiral broken bands of brown squares and blotches and, with wavy short lines below the suture. This collectors' item comes from moderately deep water and is difficult to obtain.

Other common names:
Senegalese Moon
Author of the species, form, or variety:
Marche-Marchad
Date of publication:
1957
Average size of mature shell:
2.5 cm (1 in)
Locality:
North-West Africa to Angola
Habitat depth:
Between 25 and 150 m (83 –495 ft)
Availability:
Rare

Other common names:
Starry Moon
Author of the species, form, or variety:
Hedley
Date of publication:
1913
Average size of mature shell:
3.5 cm (1¼ in)
Locality:
Western Pacific
Habitat depth:
Extends to about 25 m (83 ft)
Availability:
Common

Natica · Grayi

Description

A tiny shell, it is pale grey in colour, with three or four spiral off-white or cream bands marked with brown spots. The aperture is cream, as is the very large funicular pad. The operculum is virtually flat and has a single groove near the outer edge. There is fine radial grooving below the sutures. It inhabits moderately deep water.

Other common names:
  Gray's Moon
Author of the species, form, or variety:
  Philippi
Date of publication:
  1852
Average size of mature shell:
  1.5 cm (¾ in)
Locality:
  Central America
Habitat depth:
  Between 25 and 150 m (83-495 ft)
Availability:
  Uncommon

Natica · Turtoni

Description

Another of the scarce West African species, this has similar markings to those of *N. alapapilionis,* but differs slightly in that the spire is somewhat sloping and the shell is almost twice the size. The pattern is quite similar. There is a large umbilicus and the operculum is ornamented with six or seven rounded ridges.

Other common names:
  Turton's Moon
Author of the species, form, or variety:
  E. A. Smith
Date of publication:
  1890
Average size of mature shell:
  4.5 cm (1¾ in)
Locality:
  Western Africa
Habitat depth:
  Extends to about 25 m (83 ft) and between 25 and 150 m (83–495 ft)
Availability:
  Uncommon

Natica · Unifasciata

Description

An overall slate-grey is lightened by a creamy yellow
spiral band on the whorl shoulders. The columella and
parietal wall are white, as is the funicular pad below
the umbilicus. The flat calcareous operculum bears no
sculpturing. The shells seen here come from Pedro
Gonzales Island, Panama.

Other common names:
  Single-banded Moon
Author of the species, form, or variety:
  Lamarck
Date of publication:
  1822
Average size of mature shell:
  3 cm (1¼ in)
Locality:
  Western Central America
Habitat depth:
  Extends to about 25 m (83 ft)
Availability:
  Common

Stigmaulax · Broderipiana

Description

Prettily marked with three spiral bands of dark brown and
cream on a tan brown background, this shell also has a thin
white band below the suture. Fine radial grooves are in
evidence, and there is a wide umbilicus and large funicle.
The shiny white operculum has fine radial lirae.

Other common names:
  Broderip's Moon
Author of the species, form, or variety:
  Récluz
Date of publication:
  1844
Average size of mature shell:
  3 cm (1¼ in)
Locality:
  Western Central America
Habitat depth:
  Extends to about 25 m (83 ft)
Availability:
  Common

Tanea · Euzona

Description

A globose shell with a low spire, its striking markings consist of alternating spiral bands of white with tan brown crescent shapes and fine close tan brown lines. The aperture, columella, parietal wall and funicle are all white. This particular shell is from the Gulf of Siam in moderately deep water.

Other common names:
  Zoned Moon
Author of the species, form, or variety:
  Récluz
Date of publication:
  1844
Average size of mature shell:
  3 cm (1¼ in)
Locality:
  Indo-Pacific
Habitat depth:
  Between 25 and 150 m
  (83–495 ft)
Availability:
  Uncommon

Tanea · Undulata

Description

A smallish lightweight glossy shell, the attractively named wavy moon is off-white or cream, with axial wavy or zigzag lines of light tan. The umbilicus is open but is partially covered by a prominent funicular pad. A sand dweller, found in depths to 40 m (132 ft).

Other common names:
  Wavy Moon
Author of the species, form, or variety:
  Röding
Date of publication:
  1798
Average size of mature shell:
  2.5 cm (1 in)
Locality:
  Japan to the Philippines
Habitat depth:
  Between 25 and 150 m
  (83–495 ft)
Availability:
  Uncommon

Natica · Monodi

Description

A medium-sized natica, this has a low spire and globose body whorl. It is pale brown or beige with two spiral bands of broken brown markings. There are numerous growth lines. The umbilicus, columella and aperture are white and the lunate operculum is decoratively ribbed. A scarce collectors' item.

Other common names:
None
Author of the species, form, or variety:
Marche-Marchad
Date of publication:
1957
Average size of mature shell:
3 cm (1¼ in)
Locality:
Western Africa
Habitat depth:
Extends to about 25 m (83 ft) and between 25 and 150 m (83–495 ft)
Availability:
Rare

SUPER FAMILY
TONOIDEA

FAMILY
TONNIDAE
(Tun Shells)

The tun shells are so called because of their large rounded or ovate body whorls, the spires being relatively low. Although largish shells, they tend to be rather thin and lightweight. They are carnivorous, feeding on fish, urchins, sea cucumbers and crabs, and they virtually all live in tropical seas in moderate to deep water. They do not possess an operculum. There are three genera: Tonna, Eudolium and Malea.

Tonna · Sulcosa

Description

A medium-sized species, it has a moderate spire and channelled suture. The body whorl is ovate and bears numerous rather flattened spiral cords. The periphery of the aperture is stepped and the lower edge dentate. The siphonal canal is deep and pronounced. The white shell is encircled with broad brown spiral bands. This specimen is from Central Philippines.

Other common names:
  Banded Tun
Author of the species, form, or variety:
  Born
Date of publication:
  1778
Average size of mature shell:
  10 cm (4 in)
Locality:
  Indo-Pacific
Habitat depth:
  Extends to about 25 m (83 ft) and
  between 25 and 150 m (83–495 ft)
Availability:
  Common

Malea · Pomum

Description

A very solid small tun, it is dominated by coarse low rounded spiral cords. The spire is low; the outer lip is thick and heavily dentate. The colour is a beige pink, with occasional orange or brown patches on the cords. The columella is plicate and the canal very short. The base area is cream and the interior deep orange. It lives in offshore waters.

Other common names:
  Pacific Grinning Tun
Author of the species, form, or variety:
  L.
Date of publication:
  1758
Average size of mature shell:
  7.5 cm (3 in)
Locality:
  Indo-Pacific
Habitat depth:
  Extends to about 25 m (83 ft) and
  between 25 and 150 m (83–495 ft)
Availability:
  Common

Tonna · Luteostoma

Description

A rounded heavy species, with a low spire and moderately channelled suture, it has prominent rounded spiral cords. The columella is glazed and covers part of the small umbilicus. The outer shell is creamy white, with orange brown streaks and blotches; the interior is an orange brown. A rare find, it is fished in depths to 200 m (660 ft). This specimen is from southern Japan.

Other common names:
  Gold-mouthed Tun
Author of the species, form, or variety:
  Küster
Date of publication:
  1857
Average size of mature shell:
  12 cm (4¾ in)
Locality:
  Western Pacific
Habitat depth:
  Extends to about 25 m (83 ft) and
  between 25 and 150 m (83–495 ft)
Availability:
  Uncommon

SUPER FAMILY
TONOIDEA

FAMILY
FICIDAE
(Fig Shells)

Fig-like in shape, these are thin and lightweight shells, with no varices or operculae. The spires are more or less flat and a large tapering body whorl and aperture lead to a long siphonal canal. This is a small family, with one main genus – Ficus. The shells bear little or no pattern and, apart from their graceful shape, they appear rather drab specimens to many people. Most inhabit sandy areas in tropical seas.

Tanea · Zelandica

Description

A very rounded shell, with a low spire and enlarged body whorl, it is beige or light brown , with spiral bands of broken pale to mid-brown squares or irregular shapes. The aperture and surrounding area is white. The umbilicus is closed by a large funicle. Endemic, it lives in intertidal and shallow waters.

Other common names:
New Zealand Moon
Author of the species, form, or variety:
Quoy and Gaimard
Date of publication:
1832
Average size of mature shell:
3 cm (1¼ in)
Locality:
New Zealand
Habitat depth:
25 m (83 ft)
Availability:
Uncommon

Ficus · Gracilis

Description

This is the largest member of the family, although it is rather thin and fragile. The enlarged body whorl tapers gracefully to the canal. Fine spiral and axial cords form a 'netted' appearance. The columella is smooth and centrally concave. The shell is a beige brown on the outside; the interior is a rich brown, fading to off-white at the margin of the aperture. Found in relatively deep water, this shell was fished off south-western Taiwan.

Other common names:
  Graceful Fig
Author of the species, form, or variety:
  Sowerby
Date of publication:
  1825
Average size of mature shell:
  13 cm (5 in)
Locality:
  Japan to Taiwan
Habitat depth:
  Between 150 and 500 m (495–1,650 ft)
Availability:
  Common

Ficus · Variegata

Description

A less fragile species than *F. gracilis*, this is shorter, with an almost flat spire and bulbous body whorl narrowing to a moderate siphonal canal. There are fine spiral cords, and several growth striae are usually evident. The shell colour is a mottled medium-to-dark brown; the aperture is smooth and pale mauve or brown. It is found in sand and mud in shallow water.

Other common names:
  Variable Fig
Author of the species, form, or variety:
  Röding
Date of publication:
  1798
Average size of mature shell:
  8 cm (3¼ in)
Locality:
  Japan to Taiwan
Habitat depth:
  Extends to about 25 m (83 ft)
Availability:
  Common

SUPER FAMILY
TONOIDEA

FAMILY
CASSIDAE
(Helmet or Bonnet Shells)

In total contrast to the tun shells, the helmets are solid and often very heavy, bearing strong ornamentation in the form of nodules and tuberculate varices. It is quite a large family, with several genera, including Cassis, Cypraecassis, Galeodea, Phalium Casmaria, Echinophoria and Semicassis. Some frequently used subgenera and synonymous subgenera such as Hypocassis and Xenopallium may well be elevated to full generic status as work continues on this family and, in a few instances, these new names have been used. All species prefer warmer seas where they live on sandy substrates, mostly in shallow water. They enjoy feeding on sea urchins. Some of the large species are used for the cameo industry.

Cassis · Cornuta

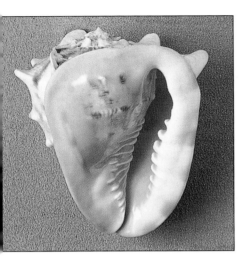

Description

The most obvious feature of this, arguably the largest and heaviest species in the family, is the deep yellowy orange shield-like area on the underside. This comprises a thickened dentate lip, which is joined at the posterior to an enlarged parietal wall and columella. It is a highly glossy area and virtually hides the body whorl when viewed from underneath the shell. There is a low spire and a large angular body whorl, heavily knobbed at the shoulder. A coral reef dweller.

Other common names:
Horned Helmet
Author of the species, form or variety:
L.
Date of publication:
1758
Average size of mature shell:
30 cm (12 in)
Locality:
Indo-Pacific
Habitat depth:
Extends to about 25 m (83 ft)
Availability:
Common

Cypraecassis · Rufa

Description

Often referred to as the cameo shell, it is this species, more so than other large cassis, which is used for the manufacture of cameos for the jewellery trade. A solid heavy shell, it is a deep orange red with rounded dorsal nodules; the lip is thick and dentate, and the columella and parietal wall are heavily calloused. It inhabits coral reefs.

Other common names:
Bullmouth Helmet
Author of the species, form or variety:
L.
Date of publication:
1758
Average size of mature shell:
15 cm (6 in)
Locality:
East Africa
Habitat depth:
Extends to about 25 m (83 ft)
Availability:
Common

Phalium · Areola

Description

A lovely shell, it is smooth, glossy and patterned with squared markings of rich brown. The ovate shell has a medium-sized spire, and several varices are present. The lip is fairly thin, recurved and dentate and there are fine columella folds. Prefers sandy mud in intertidal or offshore waters.

Other common names:
Chequered Bonnet
Author of the species, form or variety:
L.
Date of publication:
1758
Average size of mature shell:
7.5 cm (3 in)
Locality:
Western Indo-Pacific
Habitat depth:
Extends to about 25 m (83 ft) and between 25 and 150 m (83–495 ft)
Availability:
Common

Semicassis · Granulatum undulatum

Description

The Mediterranean bonnet has a high spire and is ovate and coarsely ribbed. It is thick and heavy, with rounded whorls. The very thick solid stepped lip bears about 16 prominent denticles. The columella and parietal shield are pustulate and calloused. The beige to pale brown background is decorated with random darker brown bands and a few blotches. The aperture is white, darkening to orange brown within.

Other common names:
Mediterranean Bonnet
Author of the species, form or variety:
Gmelin
Date of publication:
1791
Average size of mature shell:
7.5 cm (3½ in)
Locality:
Mediterranean
Habitat depth:
Extends to about 25 m (83 ft) and between 150 and 500 m (495–1,650 ft)
Availability:
Common

Semicassis · Granulatum granulatum

Description

A stocky ovate shell, with a medium spire, the Scotch bonnet appears relatively smooth, but on closer examination there are fine spiral grooves and faint axial growth striae. The lip is thickened, recurved and dentate, and there are numerous pustules on the columella at the anterior and on the shield. It is beige, with brown squared marks on the dorsum, and pure white on the underside.

Other common names:
Angas's Bonnet
Author of the species, form or variety:
Iredale
Date of publication:
1927
Average size of mature shell:
5 cm (2 in)
Locality:
New South Wales to N.W Australia
Habitat depth:
Between 25 and 150 m (83-495 ft)
Availability:
Common

Semicassis · Granulatum granulatum

Description

A stocky ovate shell, with a medium spire, the Scotch bonnet appears relatively smooth, but on closer examination there are fine spiral grooves and faint axial growth striae. The lip is thickened, recurved and dentate, and there are numerous pustules on the columella at the anterior and on the shield. It is beige, with brown squared marks on the dorsum, and pure white on the underside.

Other common names:
Scotch Bonnet
Author of the species, form or variety:
Born
Date of publication:
1778
Average size of mature shell:
7.5 cm (3 in)
Locality:
South-eastern USA to Brazil
Habitat depth:
Extends to about 25 m (83 ft) and between 150 and 500 m (495–1,650 ft)
Availability:
Common

SUPER FAMILY
TONOIDEA

FAMILY
RANELLIDAE
(The Tritons)

An interesting and popular family, the tritons generally inhabit warm tropical seas and are variously shaped, with much ornament. When living, the shells are covered by a thick and often 'hairy' or bristly periostracum. The varices usually bear large tubercules. The upper part of the aperture is closed, thus differing from those of the Bursidae family (frog shells), which are open at the posterior. The veliger larvae of some tritons have a free-swimming period of up to three months, and the far-flung localities in which several species occur are possibly a result of this. There has been much alteration and revision of this group. The genera and subgenera worth noting include Ranella, Argobuccinum, Gyrineum, Biplex, Cymatium, Ranularia (which has long curved canals), Charonia and Distorsio. They are carnivorous, feeding on sea urchins and molluscs.

Biplex · Perca

Description

Huge specimens of this deep-water shell used to be fished regularly off Taiwan, but this no longer occurs due to changed fishing habits. Shells half the size now come from the Philippines. The winged triton has an amazing shape – very flat with wide leaf-like axially aligned varices. It is both spirally and axially ornamented with cords and nodules. The depicted Taiwanese shell measures 8 cm (3G in).

Other common names:
  Winged or Maple Leaf Triton
Author of the species, form or variety:
  Perry
Date of publication:
  1811
Average size of mature shell:
  7 cm (2¾ in)
Locality:
  Western Pacific
Habitat depth:
  Between 150 and 500 m (495–1,650 ft)
Availability:
  Common

Ranella · Olearium

Cymatium · Vestitum

Description

As the common name suggests, this shell is found in many locations. It is thick and heavy, with rounded whorls, a tall spire and large rounded aperture. Despite the worldwide habitats, specimens differ little. The depicted shell was fished in deep water off south-eastern Italy.

Description

According to some experts, this is the Central American counterpart of the very common Western Pacific species, *C. pileare*. It is shaped in an elongated oval, with a high spire and spirally corded and noduled whorls, and is dark brown with cream or tan spiral bands. It is a shallow-water dweller.

Other common names:
  Wandering Triton
Author of the species, form or variety:
  L.
Date of publication:
  1758
Average size of mature shell:
  18 cm (7 in)
Locality:
  Caribbean, Mediterranean, Africa, Australia and New Zealand
Habitat depth:
  Between 150 and 500 m (495–1,650 ft)
Availability:
  Common

Other common names:
  Garment Triton
Author of the species, form or variety:
  Hinds
Date of publication:
  1844
Average size of mature shell:
  6 cm (2½ in)
Locality:
  Western Central America
Habitat depth:
  Extends to about 25 m (83 ft)
Availability:
  Uncommon

Cymatium · Intermedium

Description

A small stocky shell with string spirally noduled cords. The columella and parietal wall are plicate, and the inner lip is strongly dentate. The outer lip bears a heavy varix. The overall colour is orange tan, and there are darker brown markings. The aperture is a pale orange. This specimen is from Hawaii.

Other common names:
  Intermediate Hairy Triton
Author of the species, form or variety:
  Pease
Date of publication:
  1869
Average size of mature shell:
  5 cm (2 in)
Locality:
  Central Pacific
Habitat depth:
  Extends to 25 m (83 ft)
Availability:
  Uncommon

Cymatium · Perryi

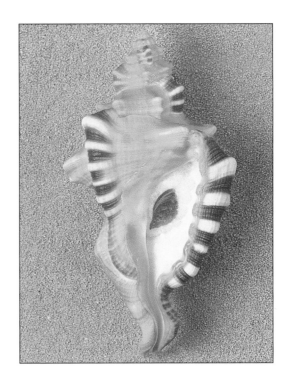

Description

Solid and heavy, with a medium spire, this species is dominated by angular knobbed whorls and rounded ribbed varices. Its colours are striking – pale orange or tan, with cream and dark brown ribs. The dentate inner lip and columella are a reddish orange. The small operculum is ovate and horny. The canal is long and curved.

Other common names:
  Perry's Triton
Author of the species, form or variety:
  Emerson and Old
Date of publication:
  1963
Average size of mature shell:
  10 cm (4 in)
Locality:
  Southern India and Sri Lanka
Habitat depth:
  Extends to about 25 m (83 ft) and between 25 and 150 m (83–495 ft)
Availability:
  Common

Cymatium · Corrugatum corrugatum

Description

A tall elongate-fusiform shell, this has coarse spiral cords with low rounded nodules, especially on earlier whorls. The lip bears very strong sharply ridged denticles, and the parietal wall and columella have fine folds. The canal is of medium length – the white shell is from Italy and the beige is from Morocco.

Other common names:
  Corrugated Triton
Author of the species, form or variety:
  Lamarck
Date of publication:
  1816
Average size of mature shell:
  7.5 cm (3 in)
Locality:
  Mediterranean and West Africa
Habitat depth:
  Extends to about 25 m (83 ft) and between 25 and 150 m (83–495 ft)
Availability:
  Common

Cymatium · Pfeifferianum

Description

An elongate-fusiform shape, it has a tall spire and long canal. Numerous beaded cords and axial riblets ornament the whorls, giving a cancelled effect. It is variable in colour, and the two forms shown here were collected off Phuket, Thailand, in shallow water.

Other common names:
  Pfeiffer's Hairy Triton
Author of the species, form or variety:
  Reeve
Date of publication:
  1844
Average size of mature shell:
  7.5 cm (3 in)
Locality:
  Indo-Pacific
Habitat depth:
  Extends to about 25 m (83 ft)
Availability:
  Uncommon

Sassia · Subdistorta

Distorsio · Reticulata

Description

The distorted rock triton has a tall spire, rather angular whorls and a short siphonal canal. There are spirally beaded cords, most prominent at the middle to upper part of the whorl. Two colour forms are shown here. The inner lip is slightly grooved, apart from which the aperture is smooth and white. This is a shallow-water species, living under rocks.

Description

A lightweight shell, its rounded distorted whorls are covered with strong cancellate ornamentation. The lip is flattened and supports both fine and coarse denticles. The aperture is complex, with parietal and columella denticles and pustules – more so at the anterior. The whole of this area to the first varix is lightly calloused.

Other common names:
  Distorted Rock Triton
Author of the species, form or variety:
  Lamarck
Date of publication:
  1822
Average size of mature shell:
  5 cm (2 in)
Locality:
  Southern Australia and Tasmania
Habitat depth:
  Extends to about 25 m (83 ft)
Availability:
  Common

Other common names:
  Reticulated Distorsio
Author of the species, form or variety:
  Röding
Date of publication:
  1798
Average size of mature shell:
  6 cm (2½ cm)
Locality:
  Indo-Pacific
Habitat depth:
  Between 25 and 150 m (83-495 ft)
Availability:
  Common

SUPER FAMILY
TONOIDEA

FAMILY
BURSIDAE
(Frog Shells)

A small family, very similar and closely related to the cymatiums (tritons), they are small to medium-sized shells, usually sturdy, thick walled and nodulose, with coarse heavy varices. The existence of an anal (exhalant) canal at the upper or posterior end of the aperture differentiates them from the tritons. Most are shallow-water dwellers, found living under rocks or among coral in warmer seas. They are an egg-laying family and are carnivores, some feeding on marine worms. There are three main genera – Bursa, Bufonaria and Tutufa; Crossata is lesser known, and there are a few subgenera, none of which concerns us here.

Bufonaria · Margaritula

Description

A short stocky shell, it has a medium spire and axially aligned varices. Both canals are prominent; if anything the anal canal is slightly longer. There are fine spirally beaded cords and one row of odd low sharp nodules on each whorl. It is very variable in colour – two forms are shown here. These particular specimens come from Palawan, Philippines.

Other common names:
  Noble Frog
Author of the species, form or variety:
  Deshayes
Date of publication:
  1832
Average size of mature shell:
  2 in (5 cm)
Locality:
  Indo-Pacific
Habitat depth:
  Extends to about 25 m (83 ft)
Availability:
  Common

Bufonaria · Bufo

Other common names:
Chestnut Frog
Author of the species, form or variety:
Bruguière
Date of publication:
1792
Average size of mature shell:
5 cm (2 in)
Locality:
Florida to Brazil
Habitat depth:
Between 150 and 500 m (495–1,650 ft)
Availability:
Uncommon

Description

This species enjoys sand, mud, or rocky substrate in depths to 100 m (330 ft). It has a flattened-ovate shape, with a tall spire. The whorls, which are slightly angled and concave below the suture, bear fine spiral rows of beading. There are one or two blunt nodules on the body whorl. It is pale brown, with greyish spiral bands, and the lip and lower columella are tinted orange.

Bursa · Bufonia

Description

The depicted specimen, although much encrusted, has been carefully cleaned to show the apparently pitted nodulose whorls. It is a chunky and heavy shell with conspicuous upturned anal canals and a strongly dentate and very thick lip. This species lives under corals, offshore.

Other common names:
  Warted Frog
Author of the species, form or variety:
  Gmelin
Date of publication:
  1791
Average size of mature shell:
  6 cm (2¼ in)
Locality:
  Indo-Pacific
Habitat depth:
  Extends to about 25 m (83 ft)
Availability:
  Common

Tutufa · Oyamai

Description

A medium-sized shell, with a tall spire, its angular whorls display fine spiral beading and two rows of nodules, strongest at the shoulders. The light brown background is decorated with random spiral streaks of darker brown; the aperture is white. The prominent anal canal is set obliquely to the shell axis. The depicted specimen was fished off south-western Taiwan.

Other common names:
  Oyami's Frog
Author of the species, form or variety:
  Habe
Date of publication:
  1973
Average size of mature shell:
  7.5 cm (3 in)
Locality:
  Japan to Philippines
Habitat depth:
  Extends to about 25 m (83 ft) and
  between 25 and150 m (83–495 ft)
Availability:
  Uncommon

SUPER FAMILY
EPITONIOIDEA

FAMILY
EPITONIIDAE
(Wentletraps)

This wonderful family of exquisitely sculptured and ornamented shells is distributed worldwide, mostly living in shallow water and found among soft corals and sea anemones, on which they feed. They are delicate shells, generally conical, with much axial ribbing or regularly spaced varices. Most have circular apertures and little or no colour. The opercula are corneus, or horny, thin and bear a few whorls. Over the years, there has been much taxonomic division of this moderately large family. According to Vaught, there are numerous genera and subgenera, of which Epitonium, Amaea, Cirsotrema and Sthenorytis are of note here. Where the generic placing of some species is doubtful, this book has adhered to the largest genus, Epitonium. The word wentletrap derives from a German word meaning 'spiral staircase.'

Epitonium · Scalare

Description

A world-famous shell and at one time a great rarity, it is now available in appreciable numbers, the shells coming mainly from Taiwan and the Philippines. It is indeed spectacular, comprising loose rounded whorls separated by strong blade-like varices, which are connected to each other at the open suture. The umbilicus is wide and open. Fished in both shallow and deep water, it is an alabaster white, with occasional cream tones.

Other common names:
Precious Wentletrap
Author of the species, form or variety:
L.
Date of publication:
1758
Average size of mature shell:
6 cm (2¼in)
Locality:
Japan to Northern Australia
Habitat depth:
Between 25 and 500 m (83–1,650 ft)
Availability:
Common

Amaea · Ferminiana

Description

The ferminiana wentletrap has a tall and relatively wide tapering spire with rounded whorls. The sculpturing takes the form of numerous axial growth striations and finer spiral cords, causing a netted effect. The shell is an off-white to grey beige throughout. The operculum is thin, horny and dark brown.

Other common names:
Ferminiana Wentletrap
Author of the species, form or variety:
Dall
Date of publication:
1908
Average size of mature shell:
7.5 cm (3 in)
Locality:
Western Central America
Habitat depth:
Between 25 and 150 m (83–495 ft)
Availability:
Uncommon

Epitonium · Perplexa

Description

Sometimes placed within the subgenus *Gyroscala*, this is a solidly built species, with a tall tapering spire and rounded whorls. These support strong blade-like varices which are joined at the suture. The aperture is rounded and there is no umbilicus. The colour is pale grey, with white varices and aperture.

Other common names:
  Perplexed Wentletrap
Author of the species, form or variety:
  Pease
Date of publication:
  1868
Average size of mature shell:
  2.5 cm (1 in)
Locality:
  Japan
Habitat depth:
  Extends to about 25 m (83 ft) and
  between 25 and 150 m (83–495 ft)
Availability:
  Common

Sthenorytis · Pernobilis

Description

An extremely rare and sought-after species, it is only very occasionally live-taken – usually in fish or lobster traps – and is reputed to dwell as deep as 1,500 m (4,950 ft). This specimen was inhabited by a hermit crab, and collected at 180 m (594 ft) by David Hunt, offshore, near St. James, Barbados. There appears to be no other species shaped quite like this wentletrap.

Other common names:
  Noble Wentletrap
Author of the species, form or variety:
  Fischer and Bernardi
Date of publication:
  1857
Average size of mature shell:
  4 cm (1½ in)
Locality:
  Caribbean
Habitat depth:
  Between 150 and 500 m (495–1,650 ft)
Availability:
  Rare

SUPER FAMILY
EPITONIOIDEA

FAMILY
JANTHINIDAE
(Purple Sea Snails)

These very delicate snails live pelagic lives – borne along on the surface of warm tropical open seas on a 'raft' of mucus-covered bubbles to which they are attached by their foot. They feed on other floating organisms, such as mollusc larvae and small jellyfish. Thousands are often washed ashore after rough storms. The family is very small, numbering possibly ten species in all; there are two genera, the main one being Janthina, all of which are purple in colour. Collectors and shell enthusiasts are primarily attracted by the beautiful colour of these shells, but are seldom able to find perfect specimens with intact lips.

Janthina · Capreolata

Description

A small very delicate shell, this has a medium spire and large rounded body whorl. The lip is drawn-in at the centre, creating a V-shape on its side, when viewed laterally. There are many fine axial striations. The depicted specimen was collected at Albany, Western Australia.

Other common names:
Capreola Purple Snail
Author of the species, form or variety:
Montrouzier
Date of publication:
Not known
Average size of mature shell:
1.5 cm (⅝ in)
Locality:
Southern and Western Australia
Habitat depth:
Extends to about 25 m (83 ft)
Availability:
Uncommon

Janthina ·Globosa

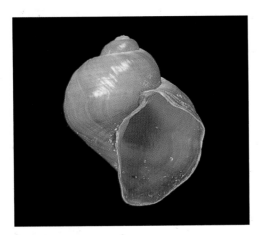

Description

Although rather like J. *capreolata* in shape the globular janthina has a lower spire, and the whorls are more rounded and bulbous. There is a similar central notch, and numerous very faint growth striations. A narrow white band runs spirally below the suture.

Other common names:
  Globular Janthina
Author of the species, form or variety:
  Swainson
Date of publication:
  1822
Average size of mature shell:
  2cm (¾ in)
Locality:
  Western Pacific and Caribbean
Habitat depth:
  25 m (83 ft)
Availability:
  Common

Janthina · Janthina

Description

The largest species in the family, the common janthina is variable in shape, some shells having a low rounded spire, while others have a medium-sized spire with almost flat-sided whorls. In either case, the body whorl is large and inflated. The specimens shown here are from northern Queensland and show the two typical shape forms.

Other common names:
  Common Janthina
Author of the species, form or variety:
  L.
Date of publication:
  1758
Average size of mature shell:
  4 cm (1½ in)
Locality:
  Worldwide in tropical seas
Habitat depth:
  Extends to about 25 m (83 ft)
Availability:
  Common

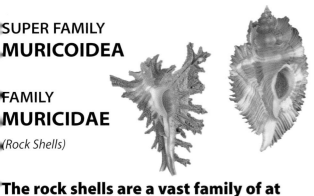

SUPER FAMILY
MURICOIDEA

FAMILY
MURICIDAE
(Rock Shells)

The rock shells are a vast family of at least 1,000 widely distributed species enjoying varying habitats, most being found in tropical seas on rocky shores, coral reefs or stony, muddy or sandy substrates. They are all carnivorous; some are able to drill holes in other molluscs, while others are able to wedge bivalves open with the use of a large projecting tooth on the outer lip. The range of shapes, sizes and sculpturing is bewildering, offering scope for many expert opinions on classification. The shells which have been chosen here are subdivided into sub-families as listed by Vaught. The rock shells, being so diverse, endear themselves to collectors and are extremely popular with conchologists. Kay Vaught lists 7 subfamilies, 98 genera and at least 50 subgenera! (The sizes quoted are for length of shell without spines.)

Bolinus · Brandaris

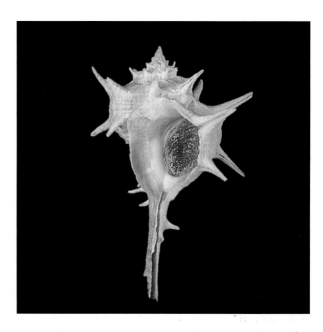

Description

A well-known species, this is one of two murex which were utilized in the manufacture of Tyrian purple dye that was used from Roman times to the Middle Ages for ecclesiastical and imperial robes. Specimens can be spinose or spineless. This is the type species of the genus *Bolinus*.

Other common names:
  Purple Dye Murex
Author of the species, form or variety:
  L.
Date of publication:
  1758
Average size of mature shell:
  9 cm (3½ in)
Locality:
  Mediterranean
Habitat depth:
  Extends to about 25 m (83 ft)
Availability:
  Abundant

Chicoreus · Nobilis

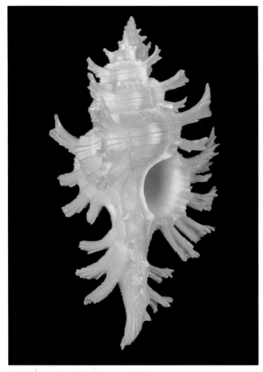

Description

A small, very beautiful shell of a deep pink colour, with fine spiral threads of mid-brown. There are three varices per whorl, and each bears medium-length frondose spines decreasing in size towards the posterior; the canal is long, slightly recurved and also spinose. The outer lip is lightly serrated and lirate within. Found in offshore waters.

Other common names:
  Noble Murex
Author of the species, form or variety:
  Shikama
Date of publication:
  1977
Average size of mature shell:
  5 cm (2 in)
Locality:
  Japan to Philippines
Habitat depth:
  Extends to about 25 m (83 ft) and
  between 25 and150 m (83–495 ft)
Availability:
  Uncommon

Chicoreus · Penchinatti

Description

A pretty little shell, this is highly variable in colour – white, cream, pale brown, mid-brown or orange. It is an elongated slender species, with shortly frondose varices and canal. There are fine spiral cords and low axial nodules on the whorls. The lip is minutely dentate. The depicted shell is from the central Philippines.

Other common names:
  Penchinat's Murex
Author of the species, form or variety:
  Crosse
Date of publication:
  1862
Average size of mature shell:
  4 cm (1½ in)
Locality:
  Japan to Philippines
Habitat depth:
  Between 25 and 150 m (83-495 ft)
Availability:
  Uncommon

Chicoreus · Cornucervi

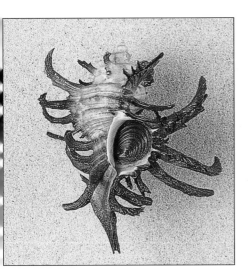

Description

A truly spectacular shell! Fully mature specimens, as depicted, are scarce, but portray the major characteristics: very strong stout long closed fronds, many recurved, some touching those on the earlier varix. The whorls are rounded and spirally corded; the lip bears a large and prominent tooth. Specimens can be white but are more usually very dark brown, with a beige undercolour. A choice collectors' item, it is endemic to its area.

Other common names:
  Monodon Murex
Author of the species, form or variety:
  Röding
Date of publication:
  1798
Average size of mature shell:
  10 cm (4 in)
Locality:
  Western Australia
Habitat depth:
  Extends to about 25 m (83 ft)
Availability:
  Uncommon

Hexaplex · Nigritus

Description

A large and handsome murex, with a low spire, it has an enlarged body whorl with about eight or nine varices and a short, wide, slightly angled canal. There are many triangular and open spines, the largest being at the shoulders. The shell is white, although the spines, large areas of the shoulders and broad spiral bands, all of which are black, can give it a dark appearance. The aperture is white. It is found in intertidal waters, but perfect sizable collectors' specimens are scarce.

Other common names:
  Black Murex
Author of the species, form or variety:
  Philippi
Date of publication:
  1845
Average size of mature shell:
  15 cm (6 in)
Locality:
  Gulf of California
Habitat depth:
  Between 25 and 150 m (83–495 ft)
Availability:
  Common

Murex · Pecten

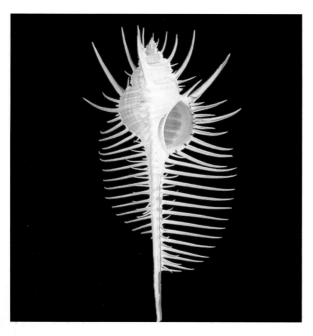

Description

The most spinose – indeed, comb-like – member of the *Murex* genus, this amazing shell is adorned with long, often curved, closed spines, and perfect specimens are collected! The whorls are rounded and bulbous, and bear numerous spiral cords. The inner lip is expanded and raised adjacent to the columella; the outer lip is minutely dentate. Pale beige to mid-brown in overall colour, it has a white aperture. The depicted shell came from the central Philippines.

Other common names:
   Venus Comb Murex
Author of the species, form or variety:
   Lightfoot
Date of publication:
   1786
Average size of mature shell:
   15 cm (6 in)
Locality:
   Indo-Pacific
Habitat depth:
   Extends to about 25 m (83 ft)
Availability:
   Common

Phyllonotus · Erythrostomus

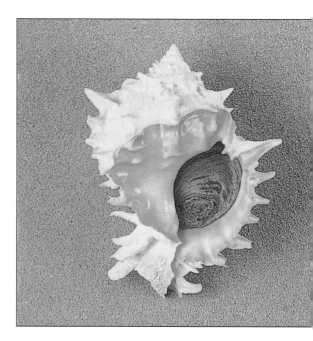

Description

A dull off-white or beige murex, it is named after its vivid pink aperture. The spire is low and the greatly enlarged body whorl bears four varices on which are blunted triangular open spines. The siphonal canal is wide and recurved. Long-spined variants occur in deeper water; the shell seen here was fished in deep water off the Californian coast.

Other common names:
   Pink-mouthed Murex
Author of the species, form or variety:
   Swainson
Date of publication:
   1831
Average size of mature shell:
   10 cm (4 in)
Locality:
   California to Mexico
Habitat depth:
   Extends to about 25 m (83 ft)
Availability:
   Common

Homolocantha · Scorpio

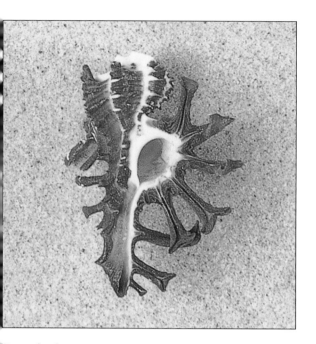

Description

This is the type species of the genus, and is a shell with unusual sculpturing, the spire being low and rather flat, often encrusted or part eroded. The body whorl is enlarged and there is a long straight canal. The suture is impressed, and there is a pit at the suture behind each varix. The varices bear long open spines; those on the lip, which are the largest, are flattened and rather flared. Shells can be white, but are more usually dark brown to black, apex and aperture being white.

Other common names:
  Scorpion Murex
Author of the species, form or variety:
  L.
Date of publication:
  1758
Average size of mature shell:
  5 cm (2 in)
Locality:
  South-West Pacific
Habitat depth:
  Extends to about 25 m (83 ft)
Availability:
  Common

Murexiella · Bojadorensis

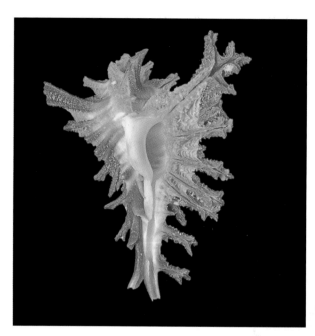

Description

A sought-after collectors' item from offshore waters, this has a low spire, long straight canal and four or five strong varices. The coarse spines are scaly and those at the shoulders are thickest and longest, the extremities being foliated and recurved. Specimens can be off-white, cream or mid-to-dark brown.

Other common names:
  None
Author of the species, form or variety:
  Locard
Date of publication:
  1897
Average size of mature shell:
  4.5 cm (1¾in)
Locality:
  West Africa
Habitat depth:
  Extends to about 25 m (83 ft) and
  between 25 and150 m (83–495 ft)
Availability:
  Rare

Ceratostoma · Burnetti

Description

A strong ovate species, this has distinctive flaring winged varices. There are low rounded spiral cords which extend onto each varix, causing an undulating effect. The outer lip is denticulate, with one particularly long labial tooth – these also occur on earlier varices. It is a much sought-after collectors' shell, from shallow waters.

Other common names:
  Burnett's Murex
Author of the species, form or variety:
  Adams and Reeve
Date of publication:
  1849
Average size of mature shell:
  10 cm (4 in)
Locality:
  Japan, Korea and South-East China
Habitat depth:
  Extends to about 25 m (83 ft)
Availability:
  Uncommon

Drupa · Morum

Description

This coral-reef dweller is probably the most well known of the popular genus *Drupa*. The spire is almost flat and the greatly enlarged body whorl bears numerous low rounded nodules. The lip is very strongly dentate, the denticles being laid in groups, with those at the posterior end bifurcated. The columella is strongly folded. A white shell, with black nodules, it has a vivid purple aperture with yellowish margins.

Other common names:
  Purple Drupe
Author of the species, form or variety:
  Röding
Date of publication:
  1798
Average size of mature shell:
  4 cm (1½ in)
Locality:
  Indo-Pacific
Habitat depth:
  Extends to about 25 m (83 ft)
Availability:
  Common

Nassa · Francolina

Description

A stocky, heavy, ovate species, it has an enlarged body whorl. There are numerous fine spiral grooves and several prominent growth striae. The lip has extremely small indentations at the edge, and a low blunt nodule at the posterior. There is another blunt nodule on the parietal wall. The shell is a pale cream pink, with large blotched areas of tan; the aperture is white.

Other common names:
  Francolina Jopas
Author of the species, form or variety:
  Bruguière
Date of publication:
  1789
Average size of mature shell:
  5 cm (2 in)
Locality:
  Indian Ocean
Habitat depth:
  Extends to about 25 m (83 ft)
Availability:
  Common

Rapana · Venosa

Description

This large heavy shell has a low spire and a large body whorl with a wide flaring aperture. This species was accidentally introduced into the Black Sea when oyster spawn was deposited there, presumably from the Far East. The shell has now become a major pest, feeding on and destroying valuable oyster beds. Large specimens are popular with collectors.

Other common names:
  Thomas's Rapa Whelk
Author of the species, form or variety:
  Valenciennes
Date of publication:
  1846
Average size of mature shell:
  15 cm (6 in)
Locality:
  Japan, China and Black Sea
Habitat depth:
  Extends to about 25 m (83 ft)
Availability:
  Common

SUPER FAMILY
MURICOIDEA

FAMILY
CORALLIOPHILIDAE
(Latiaxis Shells)

Formerly known as Magilidae, latiaxis shells are an exquisite family. Many are adapted to live in and among coral stems, but there are also a number of deep-water species. Although related to the murex, they are parasitic and do not possess a radula; many live in association with sea anemones and their relatives. Much study remains to be done if all the divisions of this group are to be gathered into a logical and worthwhile classification. Recent attempts, such as that of Kosuge and Suzuke, have made a valuable start, but there is still some way to go, especially as new, undescribed deep-water species are still coming to light. Vaught lists ten genera and seven subgenera. Here, we are primarily concerned with Latiaxis, Coralliophila and Babelomurex.

Babelomurex · Kawamurai

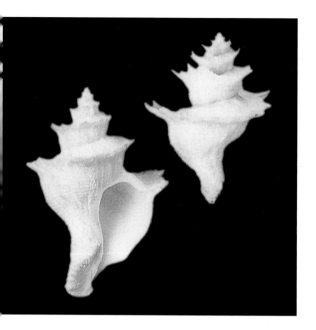

Description

This fairly widespread species is quite variable in shape – two local forms are shown here, the smaller is from Port Hedland, Western Australia, the larger was found off Natal, South Africa. Both were fished at a depth of over 300 m (990 ft). The straight-sided whorls have almost flat-topped shoulders with irregular triangular spines which extend laterally. There is fine spiral cording. This shell is always pure white.

Other common names:
  Kawamura's Coral Snail
Author of the species, form or variety:
  Kira
Date of publication:
  1954
Average size of mature shell:
  6 cm (2½ in)
Locality:
  Japan to Philippines
Habitat depth:
  Between 150 and 500 m (495–1,650 ft)
Availability:
  Uncommon

Latiaxis · Mawae

Description

A strangely-shaped and very popular latiaxis, its spire is flat or depressed, and the convex sides of the whorl taper at the anterior. The body whorl uncoils, developing outwards and downwards to a very broad expanded area which includes the gaping umbilicus and open recurved canal. The shoulders can bear triangular, frilly and sometimes recurved spines. Shells are off-white to a dirty beige in colour. Both specimens are from Taiwan.

Other common names:
  Mawe's Latiaxis
Author of the species, form or variety:
  Grey in Griffith and Pidgeon
Date of publication:
  1834
Average size of mature shell:
  5 cm (2 in)
Locality:
  Japan, Taiwan and Philippines
Habitat depth:
  Extends to about 25 m (83 ft) and between 25 and150 m (83–495 ft)
Availability:
  Common

Coralliophila · Violacea

Description

A globose shell, with a low spire, it is usually heavily encrusted and occasionally there are parasitic wormshells on the dorsum. On exposed parts, fine spiral cords are evident. The aperture is a deep violet; there are numerous fine lirae on the inner lip, and the columella is smooth. This specimen is from the central Philippines.

Other common names:
  Violet Coral Snail
Author of the species, form or variety:
  Kiener
Date of publication:
  1836
Average size of mature shell:
  2.5 cm (1 in)
Locality:
  Indo-Pacific
Habitat depth:
  Extends to about 25 m (83 ft)
Availability:
  Common

Latiaxis · Pilsbryi

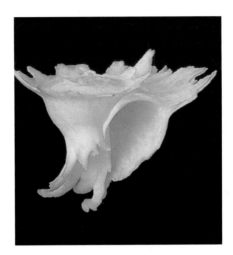

Description

This is similar in shape to L.*mawae*, but the body whorl does not stop and the depressed spire is level with its shoulders, which bear triangular spines. It is also a much lighter and thinner shell. Specimens used frequently to be fished off Taiwan. This source of supply has stopped, perhaps because of altered fishing habits, but shells are still occasionally fished in the central Philippines.

Other common names:
  Pilsbry's Latiaxis
Author of the species, form or variety:
  Hirase
Date of publication:
  1908
Average size of mature shell:
  4cm (1½ in)
Locality:
  Japan to Philippines
Habitat depth:
  Between 25 and 150 m (83-495 ft)
Availability:
  Rare

SUPER FAMILY
MURICOIDEA

FAMILY
BUCCINIDAE
(Whelks)

A large and diverse family of some hundreds of species, whelks live both in cold polar and warm tropical seas. All species are carnivorous, feeding on bivalves and echinoids. The colder-water species tend to be drab, with little colour, whereas the warm-water shells are colourful and patterned. There are many genera and subgenera, among which we are primarily looking at Babylonia and Cantharus. This family is not an over-popular group with collectors – many of the cold-water whelks, for example, come from restricted habitats and deep waters in places such as northern Russia and the Bering Sea, thus making many species difficult, if not almost impossible, to obtain; some are rather drab in appearance.

Babylonia · Spirata

Description

Although it is very similar in shape and build to *B. areolata*, the sides of the whorls are higher and straighter, and the edge of the channel formed by the suture is sharper. The columella and parietal wall are smooth and calloused; the fasciole is wide and the umbilicus is shallow. The depicted shell is from Sri Lanka and shows typical colour and patterns.

Other common names:
   Spiral Babylon
Author of the species, form or variety:
   L.
Date of publication:
   1758
Average size of mature shell:
   5.5 cm (2¼ in)
Locality:
   Indian Ocean
Habitat depth:
   Extends to about 25 m (83 ft) and
   between 25 and150 m (83–495 ft)
Availability:
   Common

Cantharus · Melanostomus

Description

A smallish ovate and coarsely sculptured shell, it has numerous spiral cords and very low broad axial ribs, strongest at the shoulders. It is a rich tan with a distinctive brown or black columella and parietal wall. The lip is dentate and there are moderate lirae within.

Other common names:
  Black-mouthed Goblet Whelk
Author of the species, form or variety:
  Sowerby
Date of publication:
  1825
Average size of mature shell:
  5 cm (2 in)
Locality:
  Indian Ocean and Philippines
Habitat depth:
  Extends to about 25 m (83 ft)
Availability:
  Common

Penion · Sulcatus

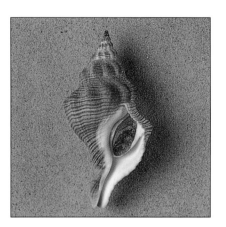

Description

This heavy solid whelk, endemic to New Zealand, is fusiform in shape, with a tall spire, angular whorls and a long open recurved canal. There are strong nodules at the shoulders, and the exterior is totally covered with coarse spiral cords. The lip is lirate, and the columella is smooth; the overall colour is beige or mid-brown, and it has dark brown cords; the aperture is white. This specimen was trawled in Houraki Gulf, North Island.

Other common names:
  Northern Siphon Whelk
Author of the species, form or variety:
  Philippi
Date of publication:
  1845
Average size of mature shell:
  10 cm (4 in)
Locality:
  New Zealand
Habitat depth:
  Between 25 and150 m (83–495 ft)
Availability:
  Common

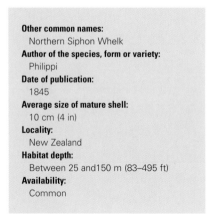

Northia · Pristis

Engina · Mendicaria

Description

A solid shell, it has a smooth texture, with the exception of the earlier whorls, which have axial ribs and spiral threads. Some authorities suggest *N. northiae* to be a separate valid species; the only difference appears to be the presence or lack of short sharp spines on the outer lip, and these differences may be a case of local variation only. The °species is found in shallow water.

Description

A tiny but solid shell, the striped engina has a spire of medium height and a large tapering body whorl. It is black, with broad yellow spiral bands. The strongly dentate lip and columella are tinged with orange or red. There are small low nodules at the shoulders.

Other common names:
North's Long Whelk
Author of the species, form or variety:
Deshayes in Lamarck
Date of publication:
1844
Average size of mature shell:
9 cm (3½ in)
Locality:
Western Central America
Habitat depth:
Extends to about 25 m (83 ft)
Availability:
Uncommon

Other common names:
Striped Engina
Author of the species, form or variety:
L.
Date of publication:
1758
Average size of mature shell:
2 cm (I in)
Locality:
Indo-Pacific
Habitat depth:
Extends to about 25 m (83 ft)
Availability:
Common

SUPER FAMILY
MURICOIDEA

FAMILY
COLUMBELLIDAE
(Dove Shells)

A large family of at least 400 species, formerly known as the Pyrenidae; the dove shells are mainly small, relatively smooth and colourful shells, living in warm and tropical seas either on the shore or in deeper water. They are carnivorous scavengers, feeding mainly at night. There are a few specialist collectors of this group, which comprises several genera, notably Pyrene, Anachis, Mitrella, Strombina and Columbella.

Columbella · Mercatoria

Description

Small and solid, this little shell has a spire of medium height and a large body whorl which is compressed at the anterior. There are fine spiral cords; the lip is strongly dentate, and the columella is plicate. The shell is white, with variable patterning and colours. The two specimens shown, which come from Yucatan, Mexico, show differing colour forms.

Other common names:
   Common Dove Shell
Author of the species, form or variety:
   L.
Date of publication:
   1758
Average size of mature shell:
   1.5 cm (⅝ in)
Locality:
   Florida to Brazil and Caribbean
Habitat depth:
   Extends to about 25 m (83 ft)
Availability:
   Common

Pyrene · Flava

Description

This little dove shell has a slightly impressed suture, a high spire and rather straight-sided whorls, making it slender in appearance. The lip is finely dentate and the aperture is long, narrow and white. The exterior colour is generally tan or orange, with one or two broad brown spiral bands and large white blotches. The shells seen here are from south-eastern India.

Other common names:
Yellow Dove Shell
Author of the species, form or variety:
Bruguière
Date of publication:
1789
Average size of mature shell:
2.5 cm (1 in)
Locality:
Indo-Pacific
Habitat depth:
Extends to about 25 m (83 ft)
Availability:
Common

Pyrene · Ocellata

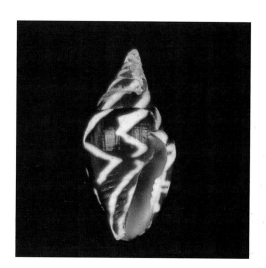

Description

Rather similar in shape and appearance to *P. epamella*, the lightning dove shell is shorter and more rounded at the centre, and its markings are more prominent – a black background with sharply defined white oblique or haphazard streaks. There is a group of four tiny denticles on the inner lip.

Other common names:
Lightning Dove Shell
Author of the species, form or variety:
Link
Date of publication:
1807
Average size of mature shell:
2 cm (¾ in)
Locality:
Indo-Pacific
Habitat depth:
25 m (83 ft)
Availability:
Common

SUPER FAMILY
MURICOIDEA

FAMILY
NASSARIIDAE

(Dog Whelks or Nassa Mud Snails)

This large family is chiefly composed of small shells which live in shallow intertidal waters in muddy substrates, though there are some deep-water species. They are carnivorous scavengers, and can detect prey at distances of up to 30 m (99 ft).In many species, the parietal shield is large and well-developed. They live together in large colonies. There are several genera and subgenera, of which Nassarius, Cyclope, Demoulia and Bullia are well known. This is not a popular collectors' group.

Nassarius · Stolatus

Description

A small, very glossy and smooth species, it has a tall conical spire and an enlarged body whorl. The lip is finely dentate; the columella is plicate; and there is one small raised ridge on the parietal wall. There are low rounded axial ribs, more prominent on the earlier whorls. Shells are variable in colour, but always appear to be spirally banded. This selection is from southern India.

Other common names:
  None
Author of the species, form or variety:
  Gmelin
Date of publication:
  1791
Average size of mature shell:
  2 cm (¾ in)
Locality:
  Indian Ocean
Habitat depth:
  Extends to about 25 m (83 ft)
Availability:
  Abundant

SUPER FAMILY
MURICOIDEA

FAMILY
MELONGENIDAE
(Crown Conch, Swamp Conch)

A relatively small family of shells, ranging in size from medium to very large, they dwell mainly in tropical regions, living in fairly shallow water in brackish or muddy areas, often near mangroves. They are predatory carnivores, feeding primarily on bivalves. This group includes a naturally sinistral (left-handed) species, as well as the largest living gastropod, Syrinx aruanus. There are six genera: Melongena, Busycon, Pugilina, Syrinx, Taphon and Volema, and several subgenera. Some are also commonly known as whelks.

Busycon · Canaliculatum

Description

The channelled whelk has a low spire, and straight-sided whorls, angled at the shoulders into a deeply channelled suture. The enlarged body whorl tapers gracefully into a long open siphonal canal. The depicted specimen, which is from Florida, has axial patterning; the colder-water shells are usually a plain pale beige to mid-brown.

Other common names:
  Channelled Whelk
Author of the species, form or variety:
  L.
Date of publication:
  1758
Average size of mature shell:
  15 cm (6 in)
Locality:
  Cape Cod to Florida
Habitat depth:
  Extends to about 25 m (83 ft)
Availability:
  Common

SUPER FAMILY
MURICOIDEA

FAMILY
FASCIOLARIIDAE
(Tulip and Spindle Shells)

A large and popular group, this is chiefly composed of shells of medium and large size, and encompasses several genera, including Fasciolaria, Pleuroploca, Fusinus, Latirus and Colubraria. Common names include the horse conch, this being among the largest in the family. Most species live in warm shallow waters and are carnivorous, eating bivalve shells and similar creatures. The family exhibits a wide variety of shapes, ornamentation, colours and patterns, Fusinus being particularly distinctive, with very tall spires and long siphonal canals.

Fasciolaria · Tulipa

Description

A large fusiform shell, the true tulip is characterized by its high spire, rounded whorls and strong open canal. It is smooth and glossy, apart from a beaded and ridged suture, and usually has haphazard patches of brown or orange and thin dark spiral bands. The lip margin is finely crenulated, and there are two or more pleats on the columella. An attractive and showy species, it lives on sand in shallow water.

Other common names:
  True Tulip Shell
Author of the species, form or variety:
  L.
Date of publication:
  1758
Average size of mature shell:
  15 cm (6 in)
Locality:
  Florida, Caribbean to Brazil
Habitat depth:
  Extends to about 25 m (83 ft)
Availability:
  Common

Fusinus · Crassiplicatus

Description

A smooth fairly lightweight species, endemic to its Australian habitat, it has whorls that are virtually straight sided, and a calloused protoconch. The lip is not thickened, and the interior is smooth apart from about four columella plaits. The patterns and colours hardly vary. This shell was trawled in Cape Moreton, Queensland.

Other common names:
Silklike Volute
Author of the species, form or variety:
Thornley
Date of publication:
1951
Average size of mature shell:
10 cm (4 in)
Locality:
Eastern and Southern Australia
Habitat depth:
Between 150-500 m (495-1,650 ft)
Availability:
Uncommon

Latirus · Polygonus

Description

A solidly built shell, with a spire of medium height and a fairly short open canal, it has strong rounded axial ribs and nodules which are usually low but sharp, and most prominent at the shoulders. Attractively coloured with dark brown broken spiral bands on a white or pale orange background, it inhabits intertidal reefs.

Other common names:
Polygon Latirus
Author of the species, form or variety:
Gmelin
Date of publication:
1791
Average size of mature shell:
7 cm (2¾ in)
Locality:
Indo-Pacific
Habitat depth:
Extends to about 25 m (83 ft)
Availability:
Common

SUPER FAMILY
MURICOIDEA

FAMILY
VOLUTIDAE
(The Volutes)

A large and very colourful family, the volutes are highly popular with collectors although they lack much elaborate sculpturing. Many are smooth and highly glossy. Most shells are of medium or large size; all are carnivorous, and the most colourful and highly patterned varieties live in tropical seas. Many inhabit deep water and are therefore difficult to obtain, which renders them much sought-after as collectors' items. Most have characteristic columella plaits or plicae and certain genera, such as Neptuneopsis, possess operculae. There are numerous genera (Vaught lists 46!), but noteworthy here are Voluta, Lyria, Cymbium, Cymbiola, Melo, Amoria and Scaphella.

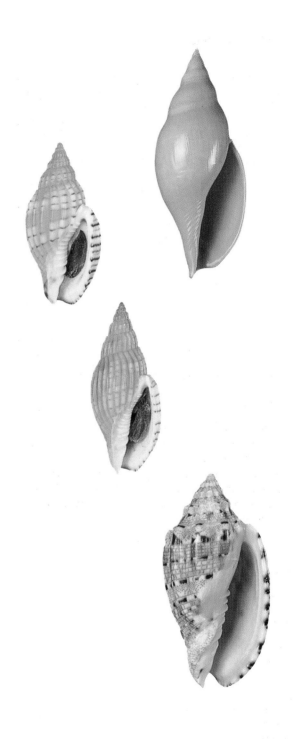

Ericusa · Sericata

Description

A popular and well-known volute among collectors, its patterns resemble medieval chant music. This robust stocky shell varies in general shape and colouring, depending on its locality. Of the two shells shown, the paler orange form was collected in Barbados, whereas the darker and more chunky specimen is from the north coast of Trinidad.

Other common names:
  Music Volute
Author of the species, form or variety:
  L.
Date of publication:
  1758
Average size of mature shell:
  7.5 cm (3 in)
Locality:
  Caribbean
Habitat depth:
  Extends to about 25 m (83 ft)
Availability:
  Common

Voluta · Musica

Description

A popular and well-known volute among collectors, its patterns resemble medieval chant music. This robust stocky shell varies in general shape and colouring, depending on its locality. Of the two shells shown, the paler orange form was collected in Barbados, whereas the darker and more chunky specimen is from the north coast of Trinidad.

Other common names:
  Music Volute
Author of the species, form or variety:
  L.
Date of publication:
  1758
Average size of mature shell:
  7.5 cm (3 in)
Locality:
  Caribbean
Habitat depth:
  Extends to about 25 m (83 ft)
Availability:
  Common

Cymbiola ·Nobilis

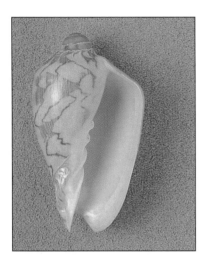

Description

This very solid and heavy shell has a high angular body whorl and a low spire, crowned with a large rounded protoconch. Old shells become coarse and calloused on eth interior and have a much-thickened lip. The depicted shell is a young specimen, fished off southwestern Taiwan.

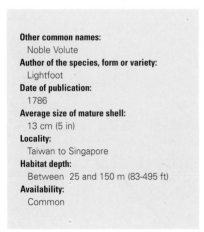

Other common names:
Noble Volute
Author of the species, form or variety:
Lightfoot
Date of publication:
1786
Average size of mature shell:
13 cm (5 in)
Locality:
Taiwan to Singapore
Habitat depth:
Between 25 and 150 m (83-495 ft)
Availability:
Common

Livonia · Mammilla

Description

The large ovate mammal volute has a conspicuous rounded and calloused protoconch. The lip is expanded and flaring. It is generally pale orange or cream, with occasional brown tent markings on the exterior and a rich orange aperture. Endemic to south-eastern Australia, it is dredged in deep waters to a depth of about 200 m (660 ft).

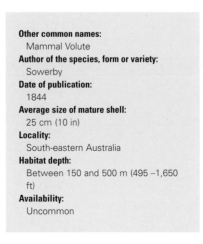

Other common names:
Mammal Volute
Author of the species, form or variety:
Sowerby
Date of publication:
1844
Average size of mature shell:
25 cm (10 in)
Locality:
South-eastern Australia
Habitat depth:
Between 150 and 500 m (495 –1,650 ft)
Availability:
Uncommon

Cymbiola · Imperialis

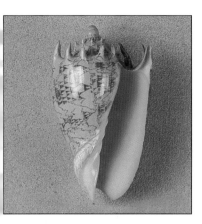

Description

A large, heavy cylindrical-ovate shell, endemic to the Sulu Sea, it has a low spire and a large rounded protoconch. The shoulders support very strong open, partly curved spines, giving the shell a coronated effect. There is a very broad calloused fasciole. The form *C. imperialis robinsona* displays identical shape and sculpturing, but has only thin non-coalescing axial zigzag lines.

Other common names:
  Imperial Volute
Author of the species, form or variety:
  Lightfoot
Date of publication:
  1786
Average size of mature shell:
  20 cm (8 in)
Locality:
  Sulu Sea
Habitat depth:
  Extends to about 25 m (83 ft)
Availability:
  Common

Harpulina · Lapponica

Description

Endemic to southern India and Sri Lanka, this is a stout volute with a moderately high spire; the whorls have high rounded shoulders. Dark brown axial wavy lines and odd dots appear over a cream yellow background. The depicted specimen is from Trincomalee, Sri Lanka.

Other common names:
  Brown-lined Volute
Author of the species, form or variety:
  L.
Date of publication:
  1767
Average size of mature shell:
  7.5 cm (3 in)
Locality:
  Southern India and Sri Lanka
Habitat depth:
  Extends to about 25 m (83 ft) and between 25 and 150 m (83–495 ft)
Availability:
  Common

Volutoconus · Bednalli

Description

This has always been a firm collectors' favourite, and large specimens command high prices. It is generally fusiform, rather broad at the centre, and its cream base colour is overlaid with unique latticed lines of dark brown. There are fine axial grooves. There is a large yellowish protoconch of about three whorls. It dwells on sand in fairly shallow water, and is endemic to the Northern Territory.

Other common names:
Bednall's Volute
Author of the species, form or variety:
Brazier
Date of publication:
1878
Average size of mature shell:
10 cm (4 in)
Locality:
Northern Territory, Australia
Habitat depth:
Extends to about 25 m (83 ft) and between 25 and 150 m (83–495 ft)
Availability:
Rare

Amoria · Exoptanda

Description

A heavy and solid shell, endemic to southern Australia, it has a large body whorl with a high rounded shoulder; the spire is low. There are three strong columella pleats and a glazed calloused fasciole. The aperture is a beautiful deep orange, and the exterior markings consist of a beige background overlaid with many fine brown tent markings and haphazard squiggles.

Other common names:
Desirable Volute
Author of the species, form or variety:
Reeve
Date of publication:
1849
Average size of mature shell:
9 cm (3½ in)
Locality:
Southern Australia
Habitat depth:
Extends to about 25 m (83 ft)
Availability:
Uncommon

Fusivoluta · Clarkei

Description

This elongate fusiform species has a tall spire and rounded whorls. The slightly thickened lip is expanded at the posterior; the columella is smooth. There are very fine spiral cords and occasional growth striae. It is pale beige throughout. A deep-water shell, it can be trawled as deep as 1,980 ft.

Other common names:
  Clarke's Volute
Author of the species, form or variety:
  Rehder
Date of publication:
  1969
Average size of mature shell:
  10 cm (4 in)
Locality:
  Southeast Africa
Habitat depth:
  Between 150 – 500 m (495 – 1,650 ft)
Availability:
  Uncommon

Scaphella · Junonia

Description

Endemic to its area, this is another choice collectors' shell, with very striking dark brown squared markings on a cream background. The shell is fusiform, with a moderate spire and long tapering body whorl. Specimens with perfect lips are scarce; they always seem to be filed. The depicted specimen was collected offshore at Apalachicola, Florida.

Other common names:
  Juno's Volute
Author of the species, form or variety:
  Lamarck
Date of publication:
  1804
Average size of mature shell:
  10 cm (4 in)
Locality:
  South-eastern USA, Florida
Habitat depth:
  Between 25 and 150 m (83–495 ft)
Availability:
  Common

SUPER FAMILY
MURICOIDEA

FAMILY
HARPIDAE
(Harp Shells)

Harps are a very small family of about 14 species and are highly collectable. They are all heavily sculptured with strong axial ribs, an enlarged body whorl and a wide aperture. The colours and patterns are exquisite. They are carnivorous, feeding mainly on crustaceans, which they tend to cover in a film of sticky saliva and sand before devouring. They are able to cast off part of their foot to avoid capture from an enemy. Most species inhabit sandy substrates in shallow water, but some rarer shells are found as deep as 200 m (660 ft). The family also includes the genus Morum, although some conchologists prefer to place these within the family Cassidae. As things stand, we have three genera to note – Harpa, the rare deep-water Austroharpa and Morum.

Harpa · Major

Morum · Grande

Description

The major harp has a large, ovate and rather inflated body whorl, with a low heavily calloused spire. There are numerous broad flattish axial ribs. The columella has dark brown staining. There is a strongly ridged fasciole. Two views of Taiwanese specimens are shown here – they display characteristic colours and patterns.

Description

An ovate shell, with a moderately high spire, it is the largest species in the genus. The exterior is very coarsely ornamented with rounded and scabrous spiral ridges, and with low axial ribs which are slightly spinose. The much-thickened lip is strongly dentate, and the calloused columella and shield have numerous low plicae. Usually trawled in deep water.

Other common names:
 Major Harp
Author of the species, form or variety:
 Röding
Date of publication:
 1798
Average size of mature shell:
 9 cm (3½ in)
Locality:
 Indo-Pacific
Habitat depth:
 Extends to about 25 m (83 ft)
Availability:
 Common

Other common names:
 Giant Morum
Author of the species, form or variety:
 A. Adams
Date of publication:
 1855
Average size of mature shell:
 5.5 cm (2¼ in)
Locality:
 Japan to Australia
Habitat depth:
 Between 150–500 m (495–1,650 ft)
Availability:
 Uncommon

SUPER FAMILY
MURICOIDEA

FAMILY
VASIDAE
(Vase Shells)

This family contains four subfamilies, Vasinae, Turbinellinae, Columbariinae and Ptychatractinae. The Vasinae are a small family of solidly built medium to large shells found on tropical coral reefs. There are possibly 25 known species. This group is popular among collectors as many are attractive and some are rare. The genera Tudicla and Afer have shells with long siphonal canals and are much less coarsely ornamented than those in the genus Vasum. Turbinellinae were formerly known as Xancinae (chank shells) from the Hindu word cankh, meaning a shell. They are a small subfamily of carnivorous snails which eat marine worms and bivalves. Columbariinae (pagoda shells) are a subfamily of deep water shells with attractive sculpturing and very long canals.

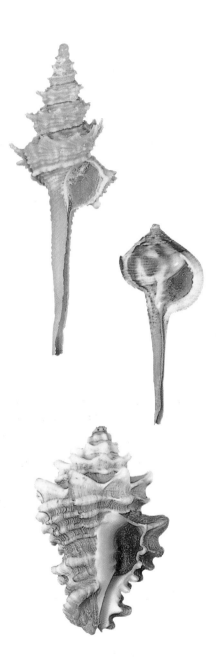

Vasum · Turbinellus

Description

This medium-sized and angular shell has a low spire and an enlarged body whorl which bears coarse nodules or, on some, spines of varying length. It is generally dark brown or black with greyish white patches, often on the spines. The aperture is cream. The depicted shell is from shallow water, Coron, Philippines.

Other common names:
  Pacific Top Vase
Author of the species, form or variety:
  L.
Date of publication:
  1758
Average size of mature shell:
  6 cm (2½ in)
Locality:
  Indo-Pacific
Habitat depth:
  Extends to about 25 m (83 ft)
Availability:
  Common

Vasum · Flindersi

Description

This is better known by its subgeneric name *Altivasum* and is possibly the largest of the vase shells. Shells are frequently trawled dead-collected, but live-taken specimens are scarce. Colours vary from white through to peach and deep orange. The spinose specimen is from Western Australia; the smaller shell is from Coffin's Bay, Southern Australia.

Other common names:
  Flinder's Vase
Author of the species, form or variety:
  Verco
Date of publication:
  1914
Average size of mature shell:
  15 cm (6 in)
Locality:
  Southern and Western Australia
Habitat depth:
  Between 25 and 500 m (83–1,650 ft)
Availability:
  Uncommon

Turbinella · Pyrum

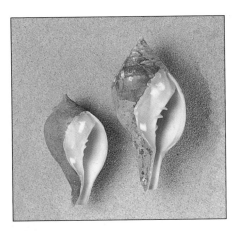

Description

This largish, very heavy shell, endemic to its area, has an enlarged and bulbous body whorl. Considered sacred to the Hindus, it is used in ceremonial and religious rites, and also in various forms of jewellery. Extremely rare sinistral shells are much sought-after and command fantastically high prices from religious Indians. Most collectors, however, are happy with a normal dextral specimen. The smaller of the two shells shown here is form *rapa*.

Other common names:
   Sacred Chank
Author of the species, form or variety:
   L.
Date of publication:
   1758
Average size of mature shell:
   15 cm (6 in)
Locality:
   South-eastern India and Sri Lanka
Habitat depth:
   Extends to about 25 m (83 ft)
Availability:
   Common

Columbarium · Natalense

Description

The smallest species of pagoda shell, it has a tall spire, long open canal, strongly corded whorls and spinose shoulders. The suture is impressed. The depicted specimen was dredged off Durban where the species is endemic.

Other common names:
   Natal Pagoda Shell
Author of the species, form or variety:
   Tomlin
Date of publication:
   1928
Average size of mature shell:
   4 cm (1½ in)
Locality:
   Durban, South Africa
Habitat depth:
   Between 25 and 150 m (83-495 ft)
Availability:
   Rare

SUPER FAMILY
MURICOIDEA

FAMILY
OLIVIDAE
(Olive Shells)

Members of this large group of small to medium-sized carnivorous gastropods are generally found in shallow water in warm tropical seas. The main genera are Oliva, Olivancillaria, Ancilla, Amalda, Olivella and Agaronia. Most species have smooth and glossy shells, and are often highly coloured or patterned. There has been a recent upsurge of interest in the true olives (genus Oliva) due to the publication of various books on the group. Many collectors despair of collecting this genus, as the patterns and markings are so very variable. However, the shape of the shell always remains consistent within the species, so for identification, shapes ought to be considered prior to markings. Most species lie hidden under sand during the day; they become active and feed at night.

Oliva · Porphyria

Description

This very handsome and attractive shell is the largest in the genus. It has a very low spire with a sharp protoconch; the suture is channelled. The body whorl is very large, elongated and rather bulbous, especially at the centre. The columella is calloused, thickened and strongly plicate, and there is a broad, flat fasciole. The colour is a pale violet pinkish tone, overlaid with rich brown tent markings, often closely arranged.

Other common names:
   Tent Olive
Author of the species, form or variety:
   L.
Date of publication:
   1758
Average size of mature shell:
   10 cm (4 in)
Locality:
   Western Central America
Habitat depth:
   Extends to about 25 m (83 ft)
Availability:
   Uncommon

Oliva · Tigrina

Description

Virtually identical to its more common counterpart *O. tigrina*, this colour form is distinctly different in that there is no evidence of dots or tent marks, the shell being completely or mostly a dark greyish black; sometimes there are broken spiral bands of cream or off-white. The aperture is white as is the columella apart from its base, which is tinged with salmon. Both shells here are from Mozambique.

Other common names:
  Black Tiger Olive
Author of the species, form or variety:
  Marrat
Date of publication:
  1871
Average size of mature shell:
  5 cm (2 in)
Locality:
  Indian Ocean
Habitat depth:
  Extends to about 25 m (83 ft)
Availability:
  Uncommon

Oliva · Vidua

Description

This olive comes in many named colour forms, but the shape varies little. It is a large shell, elongated, slightly ovate and somewhat swollen at the posterior. The spire is usually flat, and there is a distinctive calloused ridge at the posterior end of the aperture on the columella side. Shells are dark brown or black, with a white aperture.

Other common names:
  Black Olive
Author of the species, form or variety:
  Röding
Date of publication:
  1798
Average size of mature shell:
  5.5 cm (2¼ in)
Locality:
  Indo-Pacific
Habitat depth:
  Extends to about 25 m (83 ft)
Availability:
  Common

Olivancillaria · **Gibbosa**

Description

A solid heavy shell, endemic to southern India and Sri Lanka, it has an enlarged and inflated body whorl. The moderately tall spire is calloused and this extends around the suture to a thickened parietal wall, and finally down to a plaited columella. The lip margin is thin. Shells are usually greyish, with a broad band of streaked brown and yellow above the fasciole. A pale orange form occurs occasionally.

Other common names:
  Gibbose Olive
Author of the species, form or variety:
  Born
Date of publication:
  1778
Average size of mature shell:
  5 cm (2 in)
Locality:
  Southern India and Sri Lanka
Habitat depth:
  Extends to about 25 m (83 ft)
Availability:
  Common

Ancilla · **Cingulata**

Description

Also popularly known by its synonym, *A. valesiana,* this is a very lightweight and thin shell with rounded glossy whorls and a tall spire. The shoulders are slightly angled below the suture. The early whorls are a rich honey or amber colour, as is the fasciole. The apex and body whorl shoulder are white, and the rest of the shell is a pinkish cream. There are extremely fine axial striae and spiral threads. This shell is endemic to eastern and south-eastern Australia.

Other common names:
  Honey-banded Ancilla
Author of the species, form or variety:
  Sowerby
Date of publication:
  1830
Average size of mature shell:
  9 cm (3½ in)
Locality:
  Eastern and South-eastern Australia
Habitat depth:
  Extends to about 25 m (83 ft)
Availability:
  Common

Ancilla · Mauritiana

Description

A lightweight and globose species, it has a very low rounded and calloused spire and a much enlarged body whorl. The exterior colours vary from white through to dark brown. The aperture is white. The columella is slightly twisted and there is a broad fasciole.

Other common names:
  Mauritian Ancilla
Author of the species, form or variety:
  Sowerby
Date of publication:
  1830
Average size of mature shell:
  5 cm (2 in)
Locality:
  Western Indian Ocean
Habitat depth:
  Extends to about 25 m (83 ft)
Availability:
  Common

Agaronia · Lutaria

Description

A tall and elegantly fusiform agaronia, it comes from a restricted range, possibly only Java and surrounding islands. The spire is tall, and the body whorl is inflated at the centre. The suture is channelled and a calloused area above this runs around the whorls to the tip of the aperture. The cream shell is overlaid with both distinct and hazy reticulation. There is a very broad tan and cream fasciole.

Other common names:
  None
Author of the species, form or variety:
  Röding
Date of publication:
  1798
Average size of mature shell:
  7 cm (2¾ in)
Locality:
  Indonesia
Habitat depth:
  Extends to about 25 m (83 ft)
Availability:
  Uncommon

SUPER FAMILY
MURICOIDEA

FAMILY
MARGINELLIDAE
(Margin Shells)

This very large family contains at least 600 species, mostly small or very small highly colourful smooth and glossy shells. The majority of species are shallow-water sand dwellers, found in warm tropical waters, especially in West Africa, where many occur. The lip edge is thickened – hence the name 'margin' shell. Classification is complex and confusing, but in a simplified form, the following genera are to be considered: Marginella, Bullata, Glabella, Persicula, Prunum and Cryptospira, and, within another subfamily, based on the details of the radula, is Afrivoluta.

Bullata · Bullata

Description

Apart from *A. pringlei*, this is the largest margin in the family. It is a solid, smooth and highly glossy shell, with a calloused and sunken spire and a very large body whorl which is inflated at the posterior. Its colour and insignificant markings vary little. The shell depicted was collected in the sand at 20 m (66 ft) off Itaparica Island.

Other common names:
  Bubble Marginella
Author of the species, form or variety:
  Born
Date of publication:
  1778
Average size of mature shell:
  7.5 cm (3 in)
Locality:
  Brazil
Habitat depth:
  Extends to about 25 m (83 ft)
Availability:
  Uncommon

Cryptospira · Elegans

DESCRIPTION

Virtually identical in shape and size to *C. strigata*, the elegant marginella differs in that the patterning is of broad and mid-grey spiral bands on a pale grey background, intersected by numerous axial pale grey lines. Also the lip and lower columella and fasciole area are of a deep reddish brown. It is found in shallow water in sand.

Other common names:
  Elegant Marginella
Author of the species, form or variety:
  Gmelin
Date of publication:
  1791
Average size of mature shell:
  4 cm (1½ in)
Locality:
  South-East Asia
Habitat depth:
  Extends to about 25 m (83 ft)
Availability:
  Uncommon

Glabella · Pseudofaba

Description

A beautiful collectors' item, the queen marginella is similar in shape to both *G. adansoni* and *G. harpaeformis*, but is much larger and broader. The shoulders are sharply ribbed and the lip much thickened and dentate. The shell is off-white with hazy blue grey wavy bands, on top of which are numerous vivid small black squares.

Other common names:
  Queen Marginella
Author of the species, form or variety:
  Sowerby
Date of publication:
  1846
Average size of mature shell:
  3 cm (1¼ in)
Locality:
  West Africa
Habitat depth:
  Extends to about 25 m (83 ft)
Availability:
  Rare

Marginella · Sebastiani

Description

At one time this rather large and attractive margin was always erroneously known as M. goodalli. It has a large globose body whorl and a low, rather calloused spire with a rounded protoconch. Beautifully coloured, its pinkish orange background is overlaid with numerous haphazard and large creamy beige spots. It is possibly endemic to Senegal, in offshore waters.

Other common names:
  Sebastian's Marginella
Author of the species, form or variety:
  Marché-Marchard and Rosso
Date of publication:
  1979
Average size of mature shell:
  5 cm (2 in)
Locality:
  West Africa
Habitat depth:
  Extends to about 25 m (83 ft) and
  between 25 and 150 m (83–495 ft)
Availability:
  Common

SUPER FAMILY
MURICOIDEA

FAMILY
MITRIDAE

(Mitre Shells)

Mitre shells are a very large group of several hundred carnivorous species inhabiting warm, shallow seas, although a few live in deep water. Most are colourful and attractive, and they are popular with collectors. They are generally slender, fusiform shells with tall spires, and they possess a prominent siphonal notch. There are several notable genera: Mitra, Pterygia, Imbricaria, Scabricola, Subcancilla and Cancilla. They have a worldwide distribution.

Mitra · Papalis

Description

This mitre is large and heavy, with a very tall spire and almost straight-sided whorls. The shoulders are coronated at the suture; the lip bears sharp serrations; there are about five strong columella plaits. White overall, it displays very distinctive large crimson or maroon spots and blotches. The aperture and interior are cream. It inhabits coral rubble.

Other common names:
  Papal Mitre
Author of the species, form or variety:
  L.
Date of publication:
  1758
Average size of mature shell:
  13 cm (5 in)
Locality:
  Indo-Pacific
Habitat depth:
  Extends to about 25 m (83 ft)
Availability:
  Common

Pterygia · Fenestrata

Subcancilla ·Interlirata

Description

A small, solid mitre, it is elongated and ovate, with a
ow spire. The aperture is long and narrow. There are
several small sharp columella folds. The shell is
coarsely sculptured, its low axial ribs intersected with
spiral grooves creating a nodulose texture. Shells are
variable in colour, and two forms are shown opposite,
both originating from the Honiara Reefs, Solomon
slands.

Description

A slender elongated species, it has a tall spire and
rather convex-sided whorls. There are numerous
raised and sharp spiral cords. The colour is variable,
but is often off-white to beige, overlaid with fine
axially aligned streaks of orange or brown. The
depicted specimen is from the Solomon Islands.

Other common names:
  None
Author of the species, form or variety:
  Lamarck
Date of publication:
  1811
Average size of mature shell:
  3.5 cm (1⅜ in)
Locality:
  Indo-Pacific
Habitat depth:
  Extends to about 25 m (83 ft)
Availability:
  Uncommon

Other common names:
  Ridged Miter
Author of the species, form or variety:
  Reeve
Date of publication:
  1844
Average size of mature shell:
  4 cm (1½ in)
Locality:
  Western Pacific
Habitat depth:
  25 m (83 ft)
Availability:
  Uncommon

SUPER FAMILY
MURICOIDEA

FAMILY
COSTELLARIIDAE
(Mitre Shells)

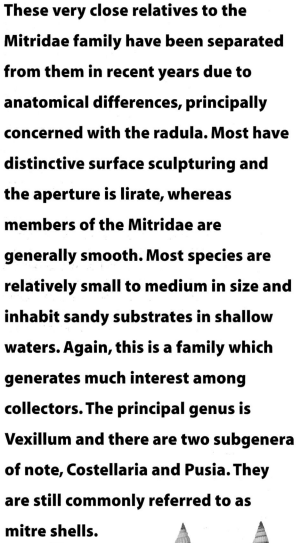

These very close relatives to the Mitridae family have been separated from them in recent years due to anatomical differences, principally concerned with the radula. Most have distinctive surface sculpturing and the aperture is lirate, whereas members of the Mitridae are generally smooth. Most species are relatively small to medium in size and inhabit sandy substrates in shallow waters. Again, this is a family which generates much interest among collectors. The principal genus is Vexillum and there are two subgenera of note, Costellaria and Pusia. They are still commonly referred to as mitre shells.

Costellaria · Zelotypum

Description

A small but solid shell, it displays coarse sculpturing of fine sharp spiral cords and rounded axial ribs which are sharply nodulose at the shoulders, creating somewhat angular whorls. The colour is off-white or cream; the anterior end of the aperture and columella are stained with lavender. This particular specimen was collected in sandy rubble on Honaria Reefs, Solomon Islands.

Other common names:
   Not known
Author of the species, form or variety:
   Reeve
Date of publication:
   1845
Average size of mature shell:
   2.5 cm (1 in)
Locality:
   Western Pacific
Habitat depth:
   Extends to about 25 m (83 ft)
Availability:
   Common

Pusia · Patriarchalis

Description

A very beautiful little shell, the patriarchal mitre is rather squat, with a stepped spire and sharply nodulose shoulders. There are numerous fine spiral grooves. As can be seen from the three depicted shells, the colouring varies; these are all from shallow water at Vairao, Tahiti. A sought-after collectors' shell.

Other common names:
  Patriarchal Miter
Author of the species, form or variety:
  Gmelin
Date of publication:
  1791
Average size of mature shell:
  2.5 cm (1 in)
Locality:
  Indo-Pacific
Habitat depth:
  Extends to about 25 m (83 ft)
Availability:
  Uncommon

Vexillum · Dennisoni

Description

This elegant and attractive shell has a tall spire and numerous low axial rounded ribs; there are also fine spiral grooves. The off-white to pinkish background is overlaid with broad bands of orange and a narrow grey band at the shoulders. The lirate aperture is deep orange. The species inhabits shallow water to moderate depths, and it is believed to be endemic to the Philippines.

Other common names:
  Dennison's Mitre
Author of the species, form or variety:
  Reeve
Date of publication:
  1844
Average size of mature shell:
  6 cm (2½ in)
Locality:
  Philippines
Habitat depth:
  Extends to about 25 m (83 ft) and between 25 and 150 m (83–495 ft)
Availability:
  Uncommon

SUPER FAMILY
CANCELLARIOIDEA

FAMILY
CANCELLARIIDAE
(Nutmeg Shells)

This family is chiefly composed of small shells living in warm seas, generally in moderate to deep water. Many are found off the western coasts of tropical America. Most are sculptured with axial ribs and spiral grooves or cords, creating a reticulated network. Few are highly coloured, and the attraction, albeit one felt by only a select few collectors, is the variable shape and the texture of the shells. Little is evidently known of the animal's feeding habits, but judging from the structure of the radula, they possibly feed on shell-less micro-organisms on the sea bed. There are numerous genera, but Cancellaria and Trigonostoma are considered to be the best known.

Cancellaria · Spengleriana

Description

This nutmeg is restricted in range to Japanese waters. It is a very handsome shell, both in proportion and sculpturing, and, as can be seen from the depicted shell, the typical nutmeg reticulated texture is evident. The axial ribbing develops into fairly sharp nodules at the shoulders. It inhabits shallow water in Japan, to which it is endemic.

Other common names:
  Spengler's Nutmeg
Author of the species, form or variety:
  Deshayes
Date of publication:
  1830
Average size of mature shell:
  5 cm (2 in)
Locality:
  Japan
Habitat depth:
  Extends to about 25 m (83 ft)
Availability:
  Common

Cancellaria · Mercadoi

Description

This very attractive species, endemic to the Philippines, has only been available in appreciable numbers during the last 10–15 years and its habitat appears to be restricted to moderately deep water in Tayabas Bay. It has been named after Mario Mercado, a shell dealer of Zimbales. The broad, raised and angular ribs and convex whorls are typical of this shell, the specimen seen here portraying the normal colouring of tan and yellow.

Other common names:
  Mercado's Nutmeg
Author of the species, form or variety:
  Old
Date of publication:
  1968
Average size of mature shell:
  3 cm (1¼ in)
Locality:
  Philippines
Habitat depth:
  Between 25 and 150 m (83–495 ft)
Availability:
  Uncommon

Trigonostoma · Scalariformis

Description

This attractive nutmeg has a moderately tall spire, convex-sided whorls and a channelled suture. There are strong rounded axial ribs. The overall colour is off-white, with broad bands of tan brown; the aperture is white. The depicted specimen was fished off south-western Taiwan.

Other common names:
  None
Author of the species, form or variety:
  Lamarck
Date of publication:
  1822
Average size of mature shell:
  2.5 cm (1 in)
Locality:
  Indo-Pacific
Habitat depth:
  Extends to about 25 m (83 ft)
Availability:
  Common

SUPER FAMILY
CONOIDEA

FAMILY
CONIDAE

(Cone Shells)

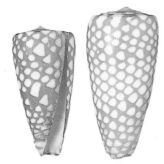

Cone shells are arguably the most popular of all families among collectors, although possibly they should be placed second to the cowries (Cypraeidae). They are a very large group of shells, small to very large in size, totalling well over 300 named species; the largest species, Conus pulcher Lightfoot 1786, exceeds 20 cm (8 in), the world size record at the time of writing being 25 cm (10 in). Cones generally inhabit warm seas, and are most prolific in the tropical Indo-Pacific; the Philippines boasts at least 185 valid species. They are a carnivorous family, preying on fish, other molluscs and worms (most cones fall into the worm-eating group). They are a highly successful predaceous family, and all species possess a specialized radula system through which a poisonous barb is injected into the prey. It is thought that the species with the largest apertures (usually fish-eating) are the most dangerous. Indeed, several human fatalities have been reported over the years due to careless handling of live specimens. All cones are covered with a periostracum when alive, and it is interesting to note that this is generally thick, so that it is virtually impossible to see any colour or pattern beneath. The true beauty of the cone shell can only be revealed after collecting and cleaning. Kay Vaught lists one major genus, Conus, and numerous subgenera. Much controversy exists among scientists and collectors regarding the systematics of this major group. There is much inter-breeding and hybridization within species, but there will always be those who enjoy creating new species, groups and variations, which inevitably adds to the already confusing array of names.

Conus · Thalassiarchus

Description

A tall, graceful shell, with a very low concave spire and straight-sided tapering body whorl, its aperture is rather wider at the anterior end. Three local variations are shown here; the slightly larger of them is the most usual colour and pattern, while the other two have had varietal names attributed to them.

Other common names:
   Bough Cone
Author of the species, form or variety:
   Sowerby
Date of publication:
   1834
Average size of mature shell:
   7.5 cm (3 in)
Locality:
   Philippines
Habitat depth:
   Extends to about 25 m (83 ft)
Availability:
   Common

Conus · Textile

Description

A most common yet beautiful species, it is popular with collectors. The textile cone has many forms and variations, giving rise to numerous names – some valid, others to be accepted or agreed upon. The smaller, 'blue' form shown alongside the typically marked and coloured specimen is known as *C. euetrios*, and has recently appeared on the market, coming from Mozambique.

Other common names:
   Textile Cone
Author of the species, form or variety:
   L.
Date of publication:
   1758
Average size of mature shell:
   7.5 cm (3 in)
Locality:
   Indo-Pacific
Habitat depth:
   Extends to about 25 m (83 ft)
Availability:
   Abundant

Conus · Eburneus

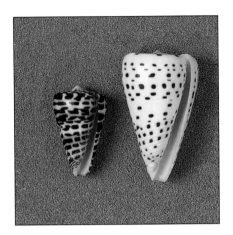

Description

A solid triangular-shaped species, it has a moderate to high gloss; the shell is smooth apart from a few spiral grooves at the anterior end of the body whorl. There are several pattern forms; the larger of the two specimens is the normal form, the smaller darker shell is the attractive variety, *C. eburneus polyglotta*. Both inhabit shallow reef areas.

Other common names:
   Ivory Cone
Author of the species, form or variety:
   Hwass
Date of publication:
   1792
Average size of mature shell:
   5 cm (2 in)
Locality:
   Indo-Pacific
Habitat depth:
   Extends to about 25 m (83 ft)
Availability:
   Common

Conus · Ateralbus

Description

An attractive shell, it is virtually black overlaid with irregular, but often centrally placed, white spots and blotches. The very low, almost flat spire is often eroded, as this part is exposed in its habitat in sand. The body whorl sides are slightly convex, tapering gently to the canal. The interior is white or tinged with greyish blue. This species is one of many endemic Cape Verde cones to have come onto the market in recent years.

Other common names:
   None
Author of the species, form or variety:
   Kiener
Date of publication:
   1849
Average size of mature shell:
   4 cm (1½ in)
Locality:
   Cape Verde Islands
Habitat depth:
   Extends to about 25 m (83 ft)
Availability:
   Uncommon

SUPER FAMILY
CONOIDEA

FAMILY
TURRIDAE

(Turrid Shells)

This is by far the largest group of molluscs, numbering over 1,000 described species, placed into numerous genera and subgenera. (Vaught lists over 200 genera alone!) Apart from taxonomic problems, the turrids are extremely fascinating, due to the complexities and variations in their shape and structure. The identification clue to any turrid is the slit-like anal notch or sinus on the edge of the upper lip. All species are carnivorous and have a venomous gland which is used in association with the radula. They inhabit all seas of the world, in both shallow and very deep water.

Drillia · Rosacea

Description

A beautiful small species, this has a tall spire, an impressed suture and a small body whorl with a short but broad open canal. There are strong, low axial ribs; the U-shaped notch is placed at the top of the aperture. The overall colour is a delicate pale pink, with darker pink tints on the inner lip and columella base.

Other common names:
Rose Turrid
Author of the species, form or variety:
Reeve
Date of publication:
1845
Average size of mature shell:
3 cm (1¼ in)
Locality:
West Africa
Habitat depth:
Between 25 and 150 m (83– 495 ft)
Availability:
Uncommon

Turris · Undosa

Description

A fusiform shell, it has a very tall sharply tapering spire and a relatively short body whorl with a moderate open canal. There are both fine and strong rounded spiral cords. The aperture, columella and canal are pale purple; elsewhere, the shell is off-white, with mid-brown streaks and patches. An attractive and popular species.

Other common names:
None
Author of the species, form or variety:
Lamarck
Date of publication:
1816
Average size of mature shell:
8 cm (3G in)
Locality:
Philippines
Habitat depth:
Extends to about 25 m (83 ft) and between 25 and 150 m (83–495 ft)
Availability:
Uncommon

Turricula · Javana

Description

A fairly large but lightweight shell, with a tall spire, it has angled whorls and a long open siphonal canal. There are numerous very fine spiral cords and a series of low rounded blunt nodules on the shoulders. Its colour varies, as can be seen from the two depicted shells; the darker specimen is from Phuket, Thailand, the larger from Taiwan.

Other common names:
  Java Turrid
Author of the species, form or variety:
  L.
Date of publication:
  1767
Average size of mature shell:
  6 cm (2½ in)
Locality:
  Indo-Pacific
Habitat depth:
  Extends to about 25 m (83 ft) and between 25 and 150 m (83– 495 ft)
Availability:
  Common

Thatcheria · Mirabilis

Description

This is a wonderful pagoda-like lightweight shell of elegant proportions. A deep-water species, it is still regularly fished off Taiwan, but in recent years large and usually paler specimens have been trawled off Port Hedland, Western Australia in about 250 m (825 ft) of water.

Other common names:
  Miraculous Thatcher Shell
Author of the species, form or variety:
  Angas
Date of publication:
  1877
Average size of mature shell:
  7.5 cm (3 in)
Locality:
  Japan to North-western Australia
Habitat depth:
  Between 150 and 500 m (495–1,650 ft)
Availability:
  Uncommon

SUPER FAMILY
CONOIDEA

FAMILY
TEREBRIDAE
(AugerShells)

This is a large family of very long and slender shells, ranging from small to large in size, and with numerous whorls. They are carnivorous and for the most part inhabit warm seas. The group arouses only modest interest among collectors, although many species are decorative and colourful. They all possess a thin horny operculum, and live in sand. Unlike many other highly glossy shells, the augers are not covered with a periostracum when living. There are eight main genera according to Vaught; but we are primarily interested in Terebra. There are also numerous subgenera.

Terebra · Subulata

Description

A tall and slender shell, its spire comprises at least 20 slightly convex-sided whorls. The suture is impressed. The body whorl, as in all augers, narrows to a short open canal. The creamy beige background is overlaid with two distinct spiral rows of dark brown squared blotches.

Other common names:
  Subulate Auger
Author of the species, form or variety:
  L.
Date of publication:
  1767
Average size of mature shell:
  13 cm (5 in)
Locality:
  Indo-Pacific
Habitat depth:
  Extends to about 25 m (83 ft)
Availability:
  Common

Terebra · Strigata

Description

A stocky auger, it has an inflated body whorl and an acute tall spire. There is one fine spiral groove below the suture and numerous low axial ribs on the earlier whorls. It is a most strikingly marked shell, with vivid dark brown axial streaks and 'flame' markings on a dull cream background. Shells often have healed breaks and growth scars. This specimen is from Gubernadora Island, Panama.

Other common names:
Zebra Auger
Author of the species, form or variety:
Sowerby
Date of publication:
1825
Average size of mature shell:
10 cm (4 in)
Locality:
Western Central America and Galapagos Islands
Habitat depth:
Extends to about 25 m (83 ft)
Availability:
Common

Terebra · Ornata

Description

A medium-sized sturdily built species, it has straight-sided whorls. The suture is impressed, and there is one spiral groove midway between it, on each whorl. The shell is matte in appearance, and the cream background is decorated with spiral rows of neat hazy brown spots. A sought-after collectors' shell.

Other common names:
Ornate Auger
Author of the species, form or variety:
Grey
Date of publication:
1834
Average size of mature shell:
9 cm (3½ in)
Locality:
Western Central America and Galapagos Islands
Habitat depth:
Extends to about 25 m (83 ft) and between 25 and 150 m (83–495 ft)
Availability:
Uncommon

SUPER FAMILY
ARCHITECTONICOIDEA

FAMILY
ARCHITECTONICIDAE
(Sundial Shells)

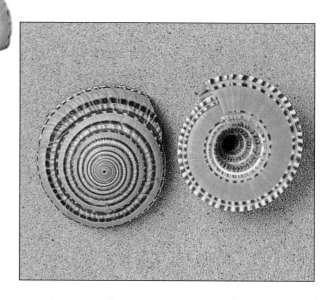

Architectonica · Perspectiva

This is a small family of flat, disc-shaped shells, with low spires, and a sharply keeled periphery; they have a large and open umbilicus. They possess a horny operculum and inhabit varying depths of water, generally in tropical seas. There are several genera, of which only Architectonica, is of interest to us. Differences between the larger species are not easy to detect by pattern and markings alone; more study is required before the collector can satisfactorily differentiate between them – no one handbook or guide facilitates quick identification of this rather confusing group.

Description

A large solid shell, it has a low spire and a flat base. On each whorl is one deep spiral groove below the suture and one strong raised cord above. There are two raised cords above the periphery keel of the body whorl. There are numerous fine axial grooves on the earlier whorls. Two beaded ridges and one groove border the wide and deep umbilicus. The species is a shallow-water sand dweller.

Other common names:
  Clear Sundial
Author of the species, form or variety:
  L.
Date of publication:
  1758
Average size of mature shell:
  5.5 cm (2¼ in)
Locality:
  Indo-Pacific
Habitat depth:
  Extends to about 25 m (83 ft)
Availability:
  Abundant

SUPER FAMILY
PHILINOIDEA

The subclass Opishobranchia comprises a group of molluscs which are mostly shell-less and without an operculum. This group includes the sea hares (Aplysiidae) and sea slugs, Nudibranchs, and generally do not concern us here. There are, however, within this section species which do possess shells and are of interest to the conchologist and amateur collector, namely the bubble shells. The families that are of interest are Acteonidae, with several genera, including Acteon and Pupa; Hydantinidae, with the genus Hydatina and subgenus Aplustrum; Bullidae, with the genus Bulla; and finally Hamineidae, with the genus Atys. They are all small-to-medium, lightweight, rounded or ovate shells, with a wide distribution. For the following species, the family heading is given but not discussed, after which the genus and species are described as normal.

FAMILY
ACTEONIDAE

Acteon · Eloisae

Description

This beautifully marked and most desirable species has a fairly strong ovate shell, with a low spire. The suture is channelled, and there are many low spiral cords. It is pure white, with vivid reddish-tan blotches, encircled with black. The species is endemic to Oman.

Other common names:
  Eloise's Acteon
Author of the species, form or variety:
  Abbott
Date of publication:
  1973
Average size of mature shell:
  3 cm (1¼ in)
Locality:
  Oman
Habitat depth:
  Extends to about 25 m (83 ft)
Availability:
  Uncommon

Acteon · Virgatus

Description

A stocky little shell, it is ovate in shape and has a low spire. The body whorl is much enlarged. It is patterned with wavy axial brown lines on a creamy white background. There are extremely fine spiral grooves at the lower end of the body whorl. The depicted shell is from Efate, New Hebrides.

Other common names:
  Striped Acteon
Author of the species, form or variety:
  Reeve
Date of publication:
  1842
Average size of mature shell:
  2.5 cm (1 in)
Locality:
  South-West Pacific
Habitat depth:
  Extends to about 25 m (83 ft) and between 25 and 150 m (83–495 ft)
Availability:
  Rare

FAMILY HYDATINIDAE

Aplustrum · Amplustre

Description

An attractive bubble, this mollusc has an ovate shape and a flat spire; the suture is channelled. The shell is patterned with two broad pink and four thin black spiral bands on a white background. This particular specimen displays good colour; many are unfortunately very dull in appearance.

Other common names:
  Royal Paper Bubble
Author of the species, form or variety:
  L.
Date of publication:
  1758
Average size of mature shell:
  2.5 cm (1 in)
Locality:
  Indo-Pacific
Habitat depth:
  Extends to about 25 m (83 ft)
Availability:
  Uncommon

FAMILY
BULLIDAE

Bulla · Striata

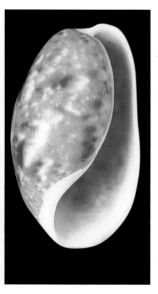
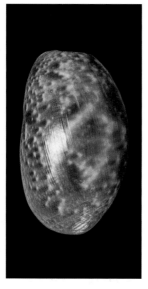

Description

This fairly sturdy bubble shell is usually ovate, with a depressed spire. The body whorl is compressed at the posterior end. Shells are most variable in pattern and colour, but all have white, brown and grey hazy blotches; the aperture is white. These two pretty specimens were collected off Yucatan, Mexico.

Other common names:
  Common Atlantic Bubble
Author of the species, form or variety:
  Bruguière
Date of publication:
  1792
Average size of mature shell:
  3 cm (1¼ in)
Locality:
  Florida to Brazil and
  Mediterranean
Habitat depth:
  Extends to about 25 m (83 ft)
Availability:
  Abundant

Acteon · Virgatus

Description

This lightweight shell is white and almost translucent, with very fine spiral threads. Ot is rather globose, and the posterior lip margin extends up and over the virtually absent depressed spire. There is a small columella fold. The depicted shell is from the central Philippines.

Other common names:
  White Pacific
Author of the species, form or variety:
  L
Date of publication:
  1758
Average size of mature shell:
  4 cm (1½ in)
Locality:
  Indo-Pacific
Habitat depth:
  Extends to 25 m (83 ft)
Availability:
  Common

Class
Bivalvia

The outer shell of a bivalve comprises two pieces, or valves, which are hinged and joined by means of a supple ligament. The valves are opened and closed by means of strong muscles located in the interior. The majority of species, of which there are around 10,000, possess a large foot, a pair of siphons and a mantle. Most are sessile creatures, but a few – such as the scallops – are very active. Oysters, mussels, cockles and clams are all included in this class.

SUPER FAMILY
ARCOIDEA

FAMILY
ARCIDAE
(Ark Shells)

A medium-sized family, it contains about 200 species, most of which live in warm seas. They are heavy, solid shells, with a long straight hinge bearing a row of many fine interlocking teeth (toxodont). They usually live attached to rocks and in cliff cracks and crevices by a byssus of hair, which serves as an anchor. Most species inhabit shallow water, but a few live in very deep habitats. This is not a particularly popular group with collectors. There are several genera, of which Arca, Anadara, Trisidos and Barbatia are the best known.

Trisidos · Semitorta

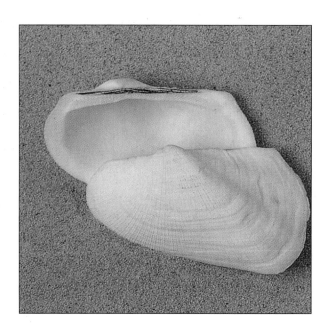

Description

This solid, heavy, chalky white species has inflated long valves which are twisted at the posterior end. There are numerous fine radial ridges and several concentric growth lines. Some shells, such as the one depicted, have a yellow interior. The hinge teeth are toxodont.

Other common names:
Half-propeller Ark
Author of the species, form or variety:
Lamarck
Date of publication:
1819
Average size of mature shell:
9 cm (3½ in)
Locality:
Japan to the Philippines
Habitat depth:
Extends to about 25 m (83 ft)
Availability:
Common

SUPER FAMILY
ARCOIDEA

FAMILY
CUCULAEIDAE
(Ark Shells)

This very small family contains one genus, Cucullaea, which consists of primitive bivalves, very closely related to the true ark shells (Arcidae). The Cuculaeidae are inflated, and one valve usually overlaps the other at the lip margin. The teeth are long and are either oblique or parallel to the hinge line.

Cucullaea · Labiata

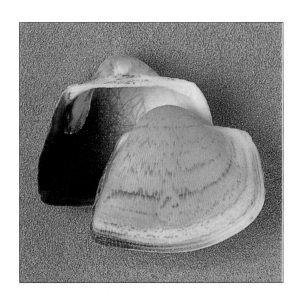

Description

A large medium-weight shell, it has inflated equal valves and low umbones. The shell is reticulated, with many fine radial grooves and crossed by concentric striations. This species can be termed a living fossil, as it has survived the passage of time over thousands of years without change in form or structure. The depicted shell shows typical colour and pattern although some have all-white interiors. It is from the central Philippines.

Other common names:
  Hooded Ark
Author of the species, form or variety:
  Lightfoot
Date of publication:
  1786
Average size of mature shell:
  10 cm (4 in)
Locality:
  South-West Pacific
Habitat depth:
  Extends to about 25 m (83 ft)
Availability:
  Common

SUPER FAMILY
LIMOPSOIDEA

FAMILY
GLYCIMERIDIDAE
(Bittersweet Clams)

These are rounded, thick and heavy shells, with toxodont teeth which are similar to those of the ark shells. There are well over 100 species, of which most inhabit shallow water in the Indo-Pacific region. The shells are porcellaneous and have a thick periostracum. There are several genera, of which Glycymeris is the best known. Many species are edible.

Glycymeris · **Pectunculus**

Description

This bittersweet has rather compressed, rounded and solid symmetrical valves, dominated by strong radial ribs. It is cream to brown, with dark brown wavy concentric bands and blotches. The teeth are obviously toxodont, and the off-white interior is stained with brown. This specimen was collected in 1 m (3 ft) of sand at Obhor Creek, Jeddah, Red Sea.

Other common names:
   Comb Bittersweet
Author of the species, form or variety:
   L.
Date of publication:
   1758
Average size of mature shell:
   5 cm (2 in)
Locality:
   Pacific and North-West Indian Ocean
Habitat depth:
   Extends to about 25 m (83 ft)
Availability:
   Common

SUPER FAMILY
MYTILOIDEA

FAMILY
MYTILIDAE
(Mussel Shells)

The species belonging to this large family occur in a world-wide range of locations, usually in shallow intertidal waters. The shells are relatively thin, elongated, and oval, with a very weak hinge structure, and a few have fine teeth. Most species live in colonies, attached to rocks by means of a byssus, but some genera burrow in rocks or coral. Many mussel species are edible. The important genera are: Mytilus, Perna, Modiolus and Lithophaga. The shells are covered with a periostracum and the interiors are often nacreous.

Mytilus • *Edulis*

Description

A well-known and most popular sea food, this species is found on rocky shorelines in great numbers, and is often farmed in 'mussel beds.' Beneath the brown periostracum is a purplish blue shell with a silver blue nacreous interior. The valves are attached by a long thin ligament. The umbones are rounded and sharply pointed.

Other common names:
  Common Blue Mussel
Author of the species, form or variety:
  L.
Date of publication:
  1758
Average size of mature shell:
  6 cm (2½ in)
Locality:
  Worldwide (not polar seas)
Habitat depth:
  Extends to about 25 m (83 ft)
Availability:
  Abundant

SUPER FAMILY
PTERIOIDEA

FAMILY
PTERIIDAE
(Wing and Pearl Oysters)

The wing and pearl oysters are a large family of bivalves living, for the most part, in tropical seas. They have a highly nacreous interior, and many are capable of producing pearls, the genus Pinctada producing pearls of gem quality. The shells grow a byssus, by which Pinctada species attach themselves to coral rubble and Pteria species to gorgonian stems. The main characteristic of the genus Pteria is a long wing-like extension of the hinge line; all species have a byssal notch (through which the byssus extends for anchorage) on the anterior margin of the lower valve.

Pinctada · Maxima

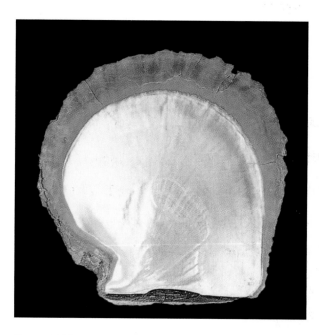

Description

This, the largest of the pearl oysters, boasts the highest quality of mother-of-pearl, and the shell is widely used in the mother-of-pearl industry. The silver yellow nacre is edged with a greenish gold tint, hence its common name. The depicted single valve clearly shows the interior, with its large muscle scar and the coarse and overlapping flaky lamellae from the exterior; the byssal notch indentation and the long hinge, to which some black ligament is still attached, can be clearly seen.

Other common names:
  Gold-lip Pearl Oyster
Author of the species, form or variety:
  Jameson
Date of publication:
  1901
Average size of mature shell:
  20 cm (8 in)
Locality:
  Western Pacific
Habitat depth:
  Extends to about 25 m (83 ft)
Availability:
  Common

SUPER FAMILY
PTERIOIDEA

FAMILY
MALLEIDAE
(Hammer Oysters)

A small curious family of bivalves, the hammer oysters have semi-nacreous interiors and a general hammer-like appearance, due to greatly extended hinge lines. The body of the shell is elongated, irregular and narrow, and consists of rough coarse overlapping lamellae. There is a small pit or indentation in the centre of the top edge of the hinge, to accommodate the ligament. Most species inhabit intertidal reefs in tropical waters. There is one well-known genus – Malleus.

Malleus · Malleus

Description

Although quite similar in shape to *M. Albus*, this is much more rugged in appearance, less regular in shape, and its extensions are rarely of equal length. The exterior and interior are a dull greyish black with a bluish nacreous area. This particular specimen, which originates from the central Philippines, has a specimen of *Spondylus* attached to its dorsum.

Other common names:
  Penguin Wing Oyster
Author of the species, form or variety:
  Röding
Date of publication:
  1798
Average size of mature shell:
  15 cm (6 in)
Locality:
  Indo-Pacific
Habitat depth:
  Extends to about 25 m (83 ft)
Availability:
  Common

SUPER FAMILY
PINNOIDEA

FAMILY
PINNIDAE
(Pen Shells)

The Pinnidae are a small family of large, thin, fan-shaped shells with equal valves. They inhabit calm, warm seas and live vertically, with their narrow end embedded in sand or mud, and anchored by the byssus to rocks and similar stable objects. The thin silk-like threads of the byssus of some species were in former times woven into very fine material – the famous 'cloth of gold.' Some museums still exhibit gloves and stockings which have been woven with this very fine substance. Of the two main genera, Pinna and Atrina, Pinna have a weak groove at the centre of each valve, whereas Atrina species do not.

Pinna · Rudis

Description

This large but thin and fairly fragile shell has sharply tapering valve sides leading to the pointed umbones. The exterior has low radial ridges from which extend upturned open flutes, or hollow spines nearer the margins. The thin shell is translucent and orange brown. The interior surface is smooth but uneven and is a nacreous silver colour at the narrow end. This immature shell was collected in Goree Bay, Senegal.

Other common names:
  Rude Pen Shell
Author of the species, form or variety:
  L.
Date of publication:
  1758
Average size of mature shell:
  38 cm (15 in)
Locality:
  Mediterranean and North and West Africa
Habitat depth:
  Extends to about 25 m (83 ft)
Availability:
  Uncommon

SUPER FAMILY
LIMOIDEA

FAMILY
LIMIDAE
(File Clams)

The file clams are a relatively large family of bivalves, the exteriors of which bear many small spines, creating a file-like texture. There are both small and large species, some living in shallow, others in deep water. They are free-swimming and highly mobile shells, moving with the help of long tentacles. For camouflage or protection some build a nest of pebbles and shell fragments on the substrate, by the byssus, which is exuded by the foot. There are several genera, the most well known being Lima.

Lima · Lima vulgaris

Description

This is a much larger variation of the *Lima lima* which is found in the Caribbean. The rough file clam is fan-shaped, with equal valves, and has a narrow hinged area and short pointed umbones. The strong rounded radial ribs bear sharp open upturned spines; the interior is smooth and has radial grooves. The shell is pure white.

Other common names:
  Rough File Clam
Author of the species, form or variety:
  Link
Date of publication:
  1807
Average size of mature shell:
  10 cm (4 in)
Locality:
  Western Pacific
Habitat depth:
  Extends to about 25 m (83 ft)
Availability:
  Common

SUPER FAMILY
OSTREOIDEA

FAMILY
OSTREIDAE
(True Oysters)

True oysters are a major food source and occur worldwide. They are generally dull in appearance, but vary greatly in shape and form. The interior is not nacreous but porcellaneous – often white or greyish. The exteriors are usually very rough and lamellate. The family is of little interest to most collectors, although Lopha cristagalli is most popular. Of the numerous genera, Ostrea, Crassostrea and Lopha are worthy of note.

Ostrea · Edulis

Description

This is the edible oyster of the gourmet and is farmed widely on a commercial basis in Britain and elsewhere. It is roughly circular, the upper valve being inflated, the lower virtually flat. The interior is greyish white and smooth; the exterior is covered with rugged layers of radial ribs and scales, and is beige or grey in colour. This specimen is from Langstone Bridge, Hampshire, England.

Other common names:
  Common European Oyster
Author of the species, form or variety:
  L.
Date of publication:
  1758
Average size of mature shell:
  7.5 cm (3 in)
Locality:
  Western Europe and Mediterranean
Habitat depth:
  Extends to about 25 m (83 ft)
Availability:
  Abundant

SUPER FAMILY
PECTINOIDEA

FAMILY
PECTINIDAE
(Scallop Shells)

Because of the diversity of pattern and colour, and also because they are easy to store, the scallops are very popular with collectors. It is a large group of several hundred species, occurring worldwide. Many are found in tropical waters, and very few in polar seas, but species occur in both deep and shallow habitats. Many species are capable of swimming by flapping their valves; usually to escape their major predators, starfish. There is a byssal notch in the anterior, on the right-hand valve. Their characteristic fan-shape remains fairly constant, but variation occurs in the surface sculpturing and the size or shape of the hinge-like 'ears' either side of the umbones. The genera are often referred to as 'pecten' by amateur collectors.

Aequipecten ·Tumbezensis

Description

As the name suggests, this is a rounded shell with inflated equal valves and ears. There are about 18 strong rounded ribs. The shells in the photograph show some of the vast array of colour and pattern variations – all of which are most beautiful. A major seafood source, it lives in subtidal to moderately deep waters.

Other common names:
Not known
Author of the species, form or variety:
Sowerby
Date of publication:
1835
Average size of mature shell:
5 cm (2 in)
Locality:
Western Central America
Habitat depth:
Between 25 and 150 m (83-495 ft)
Availability:
Abundant

Argopecten · Purpuratus

Description

This is a commercially fished, edible species. It has a large shell, its valves being equal, rounded and less inflated than those of other *Argopecten* species. The strong and fat radial ribs are a deep purple on a white background, the colours being more vivid on the upper valve. The interior pallial line is tinged with purple. A sand-dwelling species, it is found in shallow water.

Other common names:
Purple Scallop
Author of the species, form or variety:
Lamarck
Date of publication:
1819
Average size of mature shell:
10 cm (4 in)
Locality:
Western South America
Habitat depth:
Extends to about 25 m (83 ft)
Availability:
Abundant

Argopecten · Aequisulcatus

Description

A medium-sized and rather lightweight scallop, it has equal and inflated valves. It can be either fan-like in shape, or rounded, with equal ears. There are numerous strong rounded ribs. Colours vary, but the depicted specimen shows a typical form. The lower valve is usually less darkly patterned. This shell was collected at low tide in sand at Estero San José, Baja Cal Sur, Mexico.

Other common names:
None
Author of the species, form or variety:
Carpenter
Date of publication:
1864
Average size of mature shell:
7.5 cm (3 in)
Locality:
Western Central America
Habitat depth:
Extends to about 25 m (83 ft)
Availability:
Uncommon

Chlamys · Delicatula

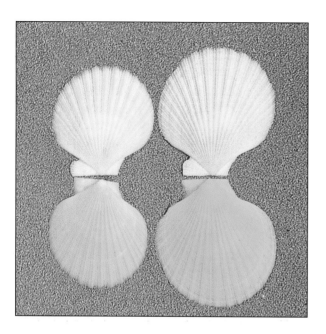

Description

A fine, delicate and very thin species, endemic to New Zealand, it is rounded, with equal compressed valves and unequal ears. There are numerous strong and coarse radial ribs. The interior is white, and although variable in exterior colour, shells are most commonly beige to lemon yellow. The lower valve is usually white.

Other common names:
  Delicate Scallop
Author of the species, form or variety:
  Hutton
Date of publication:
  1873
Average size of mature shell:
  5 cm (2 in)
Locality:
  New Zealand
Habitat depth:
  Extends to about 25 m (83 ft)
Availability:
  Common

Lyropecten · Nodosa

Description

This remarkable species has fan-shaped equal valves with about eight very large fine rounded radial ribs, often bearing large rounded nodular protuberances; the ears are unequal, the anterior being larger. Variable in colour, shells are generally reddish brown, but rare specimens are orange or yellow. A choice collectors' shell.

Other common names:
  Lion's Paw
Author of the species, form or variety:
  L.
Date of publication:
  1758
Average size of mature shell:
  10 cm (4 in)
Locality:
  South-eastern USA to Brazil
Habitat depth:
  Extends to about 25 m (83 ft) and between 25 and 150 m (83–495 ft)
Availability:
  Uncommon

Pecten · Sulcicostatus

Amusium · Balloti

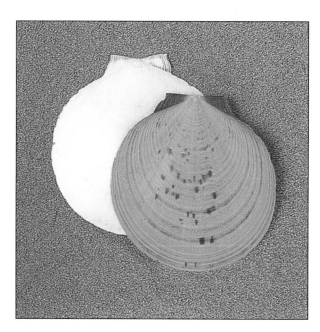

Description

This is the largest of the few South African scallops. It is fan-shaped, and has large equal ears and inequal valves. The upper inflated valve has broad radial ribs and very fine radial grooves; the lower is concave and has narrower ribs. Most shells are creamy white or beige with some pink or brown colouration, particularly on the lower valve.

Description

This is possibly the largest species in the genus *Amusium*, its rival for the title being *A. japonicum*. All species within the genus are more or less consistent in shape and form. This rather heavy shell has numerous reddish brown concentric lines and odd blotches on a pale brown background. The equal ears are a deep reddish brown. The species is commercially fished off the Queensland coast.

Other common names:
  None
Author of the species, form or variety:
  Sowerby
Date of publication:
  1842
Average size of mature shell:
  6 cm (2H in)
Locality:
  South Africa
Habitat depth:
  Extends to about 25 m (83 ft) and
  between 25 and 150 m (83–495 ft)
Availability:
  Uncommon

Other common names:
  Ballot's Saucer Scallop
Author of the species, form or variety:
  Bernardi
Date of publication:
  1861
Average size of mature shell:
  10 cm (4 in)
Locality:
  New Caledonia and Northern Australia
Habitat depth:
  Between 25 and 500 m (83–1,650 ft)
Availability:
  Common

SUPER FAMILY
PECTINOIDEA
FAMILY
SPONDYLIDAE
(Thorny Oysters)

A small group of highly spinose bivalves, the thorny oysters are closely related to the scallops and live permanently attached to coral and rocks. Sometimes known as chrysanthemum shells, they possess a unique 'ball and socket' hinge structure which rather resembles the human elbow joint. This family is very variable in shape, size and colour, making identification difficult for the amateur. Most species, however, are very popular with collectors, and long-spined choice specimens are much sought-after. In their habitat, these shells are covered with sponge, algae and encrustations, making collecting and cleaning difficult. Vaught lists one main genus, Spondylus, and two subgenera.

Spondylus

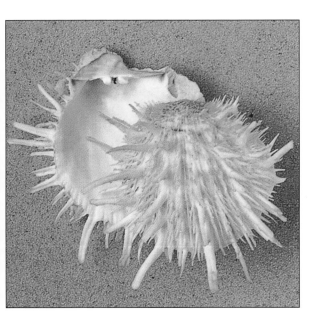

Description

A highly spinose shell, with rounded valves, it usually lives attached to coral in moderate depths. The ears are barely evident and there is a prominent escutcheon. Although this particular specimen is white, with pinkish umbonal tinting, colour variations do occur. This specimen was collected by a scuba diver off Eilat.

Other common names:
  None
Author of the species, form or variety:
  Schreiber
Date of publication:
  1793
Average size of mature shell:
  10 cm (4 in)
Locality:
  Red Sea
Habitat depth:
  Extends to about 25 m (83 ft) and
  between 25 and 500 m (83–1,650 ft)
Availability:
  Uncommon

Spondylus · Gaederopus

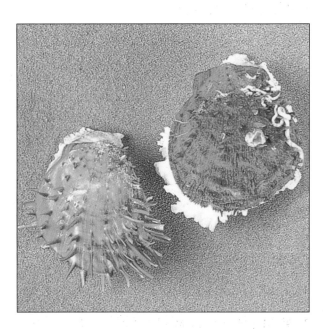

Description

A variable shell, it has more or less equal valves, but these are often misshapen. The spines can be either fairly long or short, and haphazardly placed or not present at all. The upper valve is usually coloured purple or brownish crimson; the lower valve is often white and has marine debris attached to it. The darker of the two specimens shown has parasitic worm shells and barnacles attached to the upper valve.

Other common names:
  European Thorny Oyster
Author of the species, form or variety:
  L.
Date of publication:
  1758
Average size of mature shell:
  10 cm (4 in)
Locality:
  Mediterranean and North-West Africa.
Habitat depth:
  Extends to about 25 m (83 ft)
Availability:
  Uncommon

SUPER FAMILY
ANOMIOIDEA

FAMILY
ANOMIIDAE
(Jingle Shells)

This is a small and unusual group of shells which are irregular in shape. In most species the lower valve is smaller, translucent and has a hole through \ attached to other shells, rocks, wood and other man-made objects. There are no hinge teeth. They inhabit worldwide localities, mostly in shallow waters. There are six genera, of which Anomia is possibly the best known.

Anomia · Ephippium

Description

The exterior of the larger upper valve of this rounded species is a pale grayish brown; the interior is iridescent silver green or orange. There is a large muscle scar. The small fragile lower valve is white, and has an irregular and crinkly surface; it has the characteristic hole.

Other common names:
European Jingle Shell
Author of the species, form, or variety:
L.
Date of publication:
1758
Average size of mature shell:
5 cm (2 in)
Locality:
Norway to the Mediterranean and Black Sea
Habitat depth:
Extends to about 25 m (83 ft)
Availability:
Abundant

SUPER FAMILY
ANOMIOIDEA

FAMILY
PLACUNIDAE
(Saddle and Window Pane Oysters)

This is a very small group of bivalves, with thin, often translucent valves. Some are very flat, and the adult animals live unattached; others are saddle-shaped. These shells inhabit shallow warm water and are often attached to substrate by a byssus. The species Placuna placenta (discussed below) has been widely used for many years for small window panes, and is now commercially farmed for the shellcraft industry. There are two genera, of which Placuna is widely known.

Placuna · Placenta

Description

An almost transparent pearly cream-coloured shell, it has flat valves with irregular margins. There are numerous fine concentric growth striae and the interior is smooth and glossy. The muscle scar is centrally placed, and there are two diagonal interlocking teeth. Farmed by the million for shellcraft, it is exported worldwide from the Philippines.

Other common names:
Windowpane Oyster
Author of the species, form, or variety:
L.
Date of publication:
1758
Average size of mature shell:
10 cm (4 in)
Locality:
Philippines and South-East Asia
Habitat depth:
Extends to about 25 m (83 ft)
Availability:
Abundant

SUPER FAMILY
TRIGONIOIDEA

FAMILY
TRIGONIIDAE

Many fossil forms of this ancient group are known, but there is only one recent genus: _Neotrigonia_. There are possibly no more than two species in existence, and these are restricted in range to south-eastern Australia. They are dredged offshore in relatively deep water to 50 m (165 ft) and are used in the jewellery industry for the shell's nacreous interior.

Neotrigonia · **Bednalli**

Description

This small, solid shell is roughly ovate; it is rounded at the anterior end and blunt at the posterior. Strong radial ribs bear low concentric scales. The interior is highly nacreous and can be lavender or pale orange. The complex hinge structure is V-shaped and ridged.

Other common names:
  Bednall's Brooch Clam
Author of the species, form or variety:
  Verco
Date of publication:
  1907
Average size of mature shell:
  3 cm (1¼ in)
Locality:
  South-eastern Australia
Habitat depth:
  Extends to about 25 m (83 ft) and
  between 25 and 150 m (83–495 ft)
Availability:
  Common

SUPER FAMILY
LUCINOIDEA

FAMILY
LUCINIDAE
(Lucina Clams)

A large family, it consists chiefly of white bivalves with thick and solid shells which are circular-to-ovate in shape. They inhabit both shallow and deep water and occur in a worldwide range of locations. The siphon is not usually long, so the animals make a tube to the surface with their foot. There are many genera and a few subgenera. The most well known of these are Codakia, Anodontia and Divaricella. These are not popular with collectors.

Codakia · Tigerina

Description

An attractive rounded shell, the Pacific tiger lucina has a distinctive reticulated texture of small radial ribs and concentric striations. The teeth are small for the size of the shell, but the hinge area and ligament are large. The exterior is chalky white, while the interior is a beautiful pale yellow tinged with pinkish red around the entire valve periphery.

Other common names:
   Pacific Tiger Lucina
Author of the species, form or variety:
   L.
Date of publication:
   1758
Average size of mature shell:
   10 cm (4 in)
Locality:
   Indo-Pacific
Habitat depth:
   Extends to about 25 m (83 ft)
Availability:
   Abundant

SUPER FAMILY
LUCINOIDEA

FAMILY
FIMBRIIDAE
(Basket Lucines)

A small family, it contains for the most part ovate shells which burrow into sand or mud and are generally found in warm, tropical seas. The sculpturing invariably consists of overlapping concentric and radial ribs or cords forming a reticulated surface. Several species are very attractive and are therefore reasonably popular with collectors. There is only one genus, Fimbria.

Fimbria · **Fimbriata**

Description

An ovate, solid and heavy shell, it has low flat concentric ridges and tiny radial grooves, giving a netted effect. The ornamentation becomes coarser and more bead-like at the posterior end. The exterior is white; the interior is smooth and is off-white, with a cream-tinted margin. The interlocking teeth are strong, and there is a long hinge line and ligament; the lunule is pinkish.

Other common names:
  Frilly Basket Lucine
Author of the species, form or variety:
  L.
Date of publication:
  1758
Average size of mature shell:
  9 cm (3½ in)
Locality:
  Indo-Pacific
Habitat depth:
  Extends to about 25 m (83 ft)
Availability:
  Common

SUPER FAMILY
CARDITOIDEA

FAMILY
CARDITIDAE
(Cardita Clams)

The carditas are a moderately large family of thick-walled and strongly ribbed shells, most of which are found in shallow waters around the world, except for Arctic seas; some deep-water species, however, do exist. There is a yellow-to-brown periostracum, which is sometimes hairy. The umbones are set off-centre, often well to the anterior end. Many produce and use a byssus. This group is not particularly popular or well known among collectors. Nineteen genera are listed, of which Cardita is the most widely known.

Cardita · Crassicosta

Description

An ovate and elongated bivalve, the leafy cardita has a short ligamental area. The four or so very large, low and rounded radial ribs and six or seven small ribs which are set at the anterior, below the umbones, all bear strong fluted scales. There is a large colour range, as can be seen here in these specimens fished in the Sulu Sea.

Other common names:
  Leafy Cardita
Author of the species, form or variety:
  Lamarck
Date of publication:
  1819
Average size of mature shell:
  5 cm (2 in)
Locality:
  Philippines to Australia
Habitat depth:
  Extends to about 25 m (83 ft) and
  between 25 and 150 m (83–495 ft)
Availability:
  Common

SUPER FAMILY
CHAMOIDEA

FAMILY
CHAMIDAE
(Jewel Boxes)

A colourful and very variable group of bivalves, both in shape and colour, the jewel boxes to some extent resemble the thorny oysters. They live attached to rocks or coral and inhabit shallow water, mostly in tropical areas. They grow numerous scaly plates, frills or spines, and all possess a rudimentary hinge structure. Although many species are difficult to identify, due to their great variability, several are most popular with collectors. Vaught lists three genera and four subgenera.

Chama · Lazarus

Description

This attractive shell has been included even though it cannot satisfactorily be identified. Many were collected by conchologists who served with the British forces in Gan, in the Maldive islands in the early 1970s abd U have seen many specimens, generally with little variation in colour and shape. It is probably erroneously named Chama broderippi – could it be C, *rubea* or C, *reflexa*?

Other common names:
  Not known
Author of the species, form or variety:
  Not known.
Date of publication:
  Not known.
Average size of mature shell:
  7.5 cm (3 in)
Locality:
  Indian Ocean
Habitat depth:
  Extends to about 25 m (83 ft)
Availability:
  Common

Chama · Lazarus

Description

Usually oval or generally rounded in shape, the lazarus jewel box has valves which bear very large and strong scaly lamellae, many of which extend into forked and spatulate spines. Shells are almost always white, with pastel umbonal colouring; but they can occasionally be a pale lemon colour. They are often collected in twos or threes, with attached marine debris, coral and the like.

Other common names:
  Lazarus Jewel Box
Author of the species, form or variety:
  L.
Date of publication:
  1758
Average size of mature shell:
  9 cm (3½ in)
Locality:
  Indo-Pacific
Habitat depth:
  Extends to about 25 m (83 ft)
Availability:
  Common

Arcinella · Brasiliana

Description

An attractive collectors' shell, it has radial ribs bearing numerous fine and strong spines of varying length. The interspaces have a pitted texture. The large single tooth has fine interlocking ridges. Usually pinkish beige in colour, it has a white interior. The species lives on rocks and other hard substrates, and is endemic to Brazil.

Other common names:
  Spiny Jewel Box
Author of the species, form or variety:
  Nicol
Date of publication:
  1953
Average size of mature shell:
  5 cm (2 in)
Locality:
  Brazil
Habitat depth:
  Extends to about 25 m (83 ft)
Availability:
  Uncommon

SUPER FAMILY
CARDIOIDEA

FAMILY
CARDIIDAE
(Cockle Shells)

This is a large and very well-known family, composed chiefly of edible bivalves, which live in worldwide locations in both shallow and deep water. Ranging in size from medium to very large, most species display radial sculpturing and can be either smooth, scaly or spinose. They are rounded or oval in shape, inflated and have large rounded umbones. There are numerous genera and subgenera. The genus Corculum is most unusual in that the shells are flattened, with keeled margins and overlapping umbones, and are distinctly heart-shaped. Due to their diversity of shape, form and to some extent colouration, the members of this family are most appealing to collectors.

Acanthocardia · **Tuberculata**

Description

A solid species, the tuberculate cockle has equal and inflated valves and very large rounded umbones, which in some shells touch and erode each other. There are prominent rounded radial ribs. The colour can be attractive – cream or beige, occasionally with tan to dark brown concentric bands, and with a pale orange to brown tint on the interior.

Other common names:
  Tuberculate Cockle
Author of the species, form or variety:
  L.
Date of publication:
  1758
Average size of mature shell:
  6 cm (2½ in)
Locality:
  Southern England to Mediterranean;
  Canary Islands
Habitat depth:
  Extends to about 25 m (83 ft) and
  between 25 and 150 m (83–495 ft)
Availability:
  Common

Corculum · **Cardissa**

Description

This cockle has a virtually unique form. When viewed from the anterior, it is much flattened and heart-shaped, with overlapping umbones, from which extends a sharp keel, bearing small fluted projections around the periphery. There are numerous low, slightly spinose ribs. From the posterior, the small exterior ligament can be seen, and the valve surface here is smoother and bears only fine grooves. Shells are usually off-white, but pale lemon or pink forms often occur.

Other common names:
  True Heart Cockle
Author of the species, form or variety:
  L.
Date of publication:
  1758
Average size of mature shell:
  5 cm (2 in)
Locality:
  Indo-Pacific
Habitat depth:
  Extends to about 25 m (83 ft)
Availability:
  Abundant

SUPER FAMILY
TRIDACNOIDEA

FAMILY
TRIDACNIDAE
(Giant Clams)

The giant clams are a small but well-known family of large and very large shells, the largest of which, Tridacna gigas, can exceed 1.2 m (4 ft) in length. They are a valuable sea food source; due to indiscriminate over-fishing, collecting of all species is now monitored; they are farmed in some areas. All species inhabit shallow tropical waters and live embedded in coral or rocky substrate hinge-down, so that the gaping aperture can encourage sunlight to foster algal growth within the large mantle, on which the animal feeds. There are two genera, Tridacna and Hippopus.

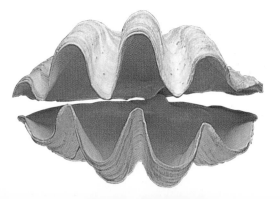

Tridacna · Crocea

Description

A rather elongated and heavy medium-sized clam, it has equal valves and broad low radial ribs which bear growth lines that are concentrically arranged and scaly. There is a relatively short hinge line and a very large byssal gape. Shells appear in a range of pastel colours, including pale yellow, or orange and yellow or cream. The interior is pure white. This species dwells on coral reefs.

Other common names:
Crocus Giant Clam
Author of the species, form or variety:
Lamarck
Date of publication:
1819
Average size of mature shell:
15 cm (6 in)
Locality:
South-West Pacific
Habitat depth:
Extends to about 25 m (83 ft)
Availability:
Common

Hippopus · Porcellanus

Description

A large species, the China clam is similar in shape to *H. hippopus,* but is more ovate and has slightly less inflated valves. The low rounded radial ribs are more or less smooth; there are many concentric growth striations. Small or young shells have a little yellow or orange colouration at the umbones; apart from this the shell is off-white. The interior is pure white and porcellaneous. This species dwells on coral reefs.

Other common names:
China Clam
Author of the species, form or variety:
Rosewater
Date of publication:
1982
Average size of mature shell:
30 cm (12 in)
Locality:
Central and Southern Philippines
Habitat depth:
Extends to about 25 m (83 ft)
Availability:
Common

Tridacna · Gigas

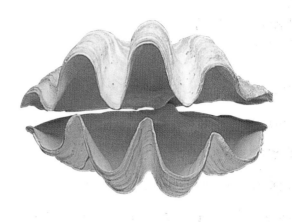

Description

This is the largest and heaviest known mollusc – the two valves can weigh as much as 230 kg (500 lbs). The elongated oval shell, with its equal valves, has about five very large undulating and rounded ribs, with numerous concentric growth striae. Mature shells are encrusted with lime deposits and much marine debris. Most shells are not particularly attractive. The interior is porcellaneous and white.

Other common names:
Giant Clam
Author of the species, form or variety:
L.
Date of publication:
1758
Average size of mature shell:
1 m (3 ft)
Locality:
South-West Pacific
Habitat depth:
Extends to about 25 m (83 ft)
Availability:
Uncommon

SUPER FAMILY
MACTROIDEA

FAMILY
MACTRIDAE
(Mactra Clams)

Mactra clams, also known as trough or surf clams, have a worldwide distribution, mainly in shallow water, and perhaps number 100 or so species. There is no byssus, and shells can either be smooth or have concentric ornamentation. There are about 24 genera, of which Mactra and Spisula are the principal ones. These shells are not popular with collectors, but many are edible.

Mactra · Corallina

Description

A smooth and lightweight shell, this is somewhat triangular in shape, with rounded margins. It is a pale reddish brown with both narrow and broad radial bands of cream. The interior is a pale lavender. The ligament is internal. It is a shallow-water species; this specimen was collected at Camber Sands, Sussex, England.

Other common names:
Rayed Macra
Author of the species, form or variety:
L.
Date of publication:
1758
Average size of mature shell:
4.5 cm (1¾ in)
Locality:
British Isles to Mediterranean
Habitat depth:
Extends to about 25 m (83 ft)
Availability:
Common

SUPER FAMILY
SOLENOIDEA

FAMILY
SOLENIDAE and CULTELLIDAE
(Razor Shells and Jackknife Clams)

These two families consist for the most part of long, narrow and thin-walled bivalves that burrow in sand or mud. Many are edible, and the species are distributed worldwide, from Arctic to tropical waters. Of the principal genera, Solen (Solenidae) and Ensis (Cultellidae) have truncated ends; Siliqua (Cultellidae) differ in that they have ovate and elongated shells, with round ends.

Phaxas · Cultellus

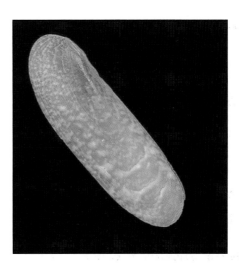

Description

Similar in size and weight to S.*radiata*, this is less broad, however, and is slightly curved, with valves that gape at the anterior end. The shell is smooth, with a moderate gloss, and is marbled with pale grey or brown on a pale lavender background. The shell pictured is from Taiwanese waters.

Other common names:
  Not known
Author of the species, form or variety:
  L.
Date of publication:
  1758
Average size of mature shell:
  7.5 cm (3 in)
Locality:
  Japan to Philippines
Habitat depth:
  Between 25 and 150 m (83-495 ft)
Availability:
  Common

Ensis · Arcuatus

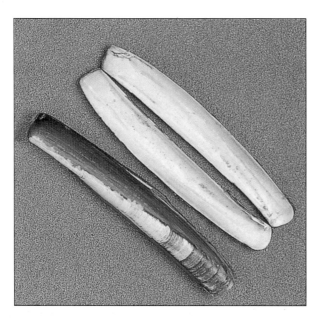

Description

This is very similar in shape and appearance to E. ensis, but it is much larger, more strongly constructed, and is either very slightly curved or almost straight. In addition, the ends of the valves are more truncated and less curved. The species burrows into sand or shell gravel from the intertidal zone down to about 36 m (119 ft).

Other common names:
  None
Author of the species, form or variety:
  Jeffreys
Date of publication:
  1865
Average size of mature shell:
  15 cm (6 in)
Locality:
  Norway to Spain; Great Britain
Habitat depth:
  Extends to about 25 m (83 ft) and between 25 and 150 m (83–495 ft)
Availability:
  Common

Siliqua · Radiata

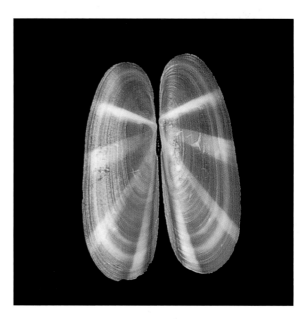

Description

A very thin and fragile shell, it is often thought of as a species of tellin. The long, narrow and ovate valves have rounded ends. There is a very small exterior ligament. This shell is a beautiful pale purple, with four broad white radial rays. It is smooth and glossy.

Other common names:
  Sunset Siliqua
Author of the species, form or variety:
  L.
Date of publication:
  1758
Average size of mature shell:
  7.5 cm (3 in)
Locality:
  Indian Ocean
Habitat depth:
  Extends to about 25 m (83 ft)
Availability:
  Common

SUPER FAMILY
TELLINOIDEA

FAMILY
TELLINIDAE
(*Tellins*)

Tellins are a family of at least 200 species of bivalves. Very small to medium in size, they are usually thin and ovate, and occur in most parts of the world in shallow water, where they burrow in sand or mud. Most are smooth and glossy, although some species have concentric lines or ridges. The umbones are very small; there are two small cardinal teeth in each valve, and the hinge plate is narrow. The best known of numerous genera and subgenera are Tellina, Strigilla, Macoma and Semele.

Tellina · Radiata

Description

This very smooth and highly glossy shell is elongated and oval. It is usually cream, with broad radial bands or rays of pink. All-cream specimens are sometimes known as T. *unimaculata*. The interior of both forms is tinged with rich yellow. The species lives in coral sand.

Other common names:
  Not known
Author of the species, form or variety:
  L.
Date of publication:
  1758
Average size of mature shell:
  6 cm (2½ in)
Locality:
  Indo-Pacific
Habitat depth:
  Extends to about 25 m (83 ft)
Availability:
  Common

Tellina · Albinella

Description

Although occasionally white, the species appears to be more commonly pink or pale orange, with fine white concentric lines. This ovate and rather elongated thin shell is compressed at the posterior end.

Other common names:
  Little White Tellin
Author of the species, form or variety:
  Lamarck
Date of publication:
  1818
Average size of mature shell:
  4.5 cm (1¾ in)
Locality:
  Southern Australia
Habitat depth:
  Extends to about 25 m (83 ft)
Availability:
  Common

Tellina · Rostrata

Description

A very thin, lightweight tellin, this is elongate and its posterior margin is rostrated. The surface is smooth and glossy, with extremely fine concentric striations. It is a most beautiful coral pink colour, deepening towards the umbones.

Other common names:
  Rostrate Tellin
Author of the species, form or variety:
  L.
Date of publication:
  1758
Average size of mature shell:
  6 cm (2½ in)
Locality:
  South-West Pacific
Habitat depth:
  Extends to about 25 m (83 ft)
Availability:
  Uncommon

SUPER FAMILY
TELLINOIDEA

FAMILY
DONACIDAE
(Donax or Wedge Clams)

These small triangular or wedge-shaped shells are a group of perhaps 50 species. They inhabit warm temperate or tropical waters, where they burrow in sand near the surface of the intertidal zone. Many are edible, some species being used in quantity in soup preparation. Of four listed genera, Donax is the principal.

Donax · Serra

Description

A large, thick species, it has equal ovate valves which are sloping and truncated at the posterior. The surface is smooth and glossy apart from the posterior portion, which has small wavy concentric ridges. The lips are finely dentate just within the shell. It is pale purple in colour, greyish at the umbones outside and purple and white inside.

Other common names:
Giant South Africa Wedge Shell
Author of the species, form or variety:
Röding
Date of publication:
1798
Average size of mature shell:
6 cm (2½ in)
Locality:
South Africa
Habitat depth:
Extends to about 25 m (83 ft)
Availability:
Common

SUPER FAMILY
ARTICOIDEA

FAMILY
ARCTICIDAE
(Arctica Clams)

This small family was well represented in prehistoric times, and there are numerous fossil forms, but there is only one recent genus – Arctica. The shells are similar to Venus clams, but have two or three cardinal as well as well-developed lateral teeth.

Arctica · Islandica

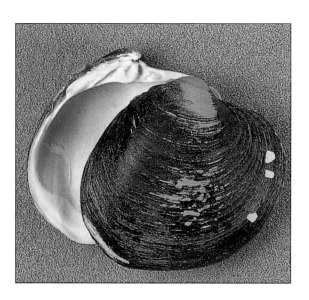

Description

A very solid and heavy shell, it has equal and inflated valves which are sometimes ovate or circular in outline. There are numerous fine concentric lines and, as can be seen here, the beige or off-white shell is covered with a thick dark brown or black periostracum. The interior is a dull white, with distinct muscle scars and pallial line. The species is an important food source.

Other common names:
Ocean Quahog

Author of the species, form or variety:
L.

Date of publication:
1767

Average size of mature shell:
10 cm (4 in)

Locality:
North Atlantic and North Sea

Habitat depth:
Extends to about 25 m (83 ft) and between 25 and 150 m (83–495 ft)

Availability:
Abundant

SUPER FAMILY
GLOSSOIDEA

FAMILY
GLOSSIDAE
(Heart Clams)

This family is a very ancient group, with numerous fossil forms, but few surviving species. The rounded inflated valves have coiled umbones, which give the shells a swollen, heart-like shape. The few known species occur both in cool and tropical seas. Due to their unusual and appealing shape, all species are popular collectors' items. There are two main genera, Glossus and Meiocardia.

Meiocardia · Moltkiana

Description

A beautifully shaped shell, it has finer concentric ridges than M. vulgaris, and the keel edges are less acute. The colour is a pale creamy white, with occasional very pale yellow tinting. The interior is pure white. A choice collectors' item.

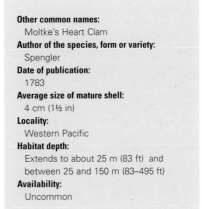

Other common names:
Moltke's Heart Clam
Author of the species, form or variety:
Spengler
Date of publication:
1783
Average size of mature shell:
4 cm (1½ in)
Locality:
Western Pacific
Habitat depth:
Extends to about 25 m (83 ft) and between 25 and 150 m (83–495 ft)
Availability:
Uncommon

SUPER FAMILY
VENEROIDEA

FAMILY
VENERIDAE
(Venus Clams)

A very large and varied family, the largest group of bivalves, containing over 400 species. Venus clams have solid-walled shells, and there is much texture and sculptural variation, making the family fascinating to the enthusiast and collector. They occur in many locations, in both cold and warm waters, inhabiting soft substrates. Most prefer shallow water, but some species live deep. Many are edible. Of numerous genera and subgenera, the notable ones are Venus, Periglypta, Chione, Bassina, Mercenaria, Pitar, Callista, Tapes, Paphia, Dosinia and Lioconcha.

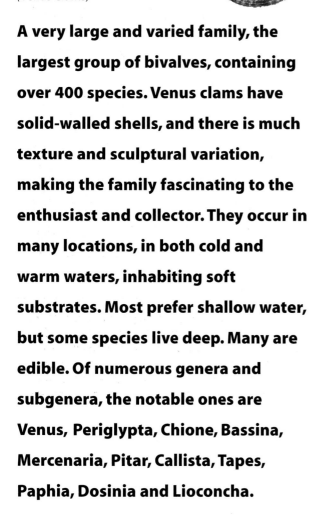

Periglypta · Magnifica

Description

The chocolate Venus clam is probably the largest and heaviest species in the family, and it seems strange that no shell-guide has included it since it was first described in Reeve's *Conchologia Iconica* back in the middle of the 19th century. It is indeed a handsome shell, with strong concentric growth lines which are crossed by very flat narrow radial ribs, giving a reticulated effect. It is pinkish beige, with dark purplish grey margins. There are very strong cardinal teeth and distinct muscle scars and pallial lines. The valves are rounded and equal.

Other common names:
  Chocolate Venus Clam
Author of the species, form or variety:
  Sowerby
Date of publication:
  1875
Average size of mature shell:
  14 cm (5½ in)
Locality:
  Philippines
Habitat depth:
  Extends to about 25 m (83 ft)
Availability:
  Common

Anomalocardia · Subrugosa

Meretrix · Lusoria

Description

The partially-rough Venus has very thick solid equal
valves with strong rounded concentric ridges. There
are two cardinal teeth in each valve. The dirty beige
background is overlaid with about four broad dark
grey or brown rays. The species lives on intertidal mud
flats and is an important food source. The larger
specimen here is from Ecuador.

Description

A thick, heavy shell, the pokerchip Venus has smooth
equal valves and a high gloss. Some are devoid of
pattern; others have brown rays or zigzag lines. The
specimen in the photograph has pale grey rays on a
creamy grey background. The interior is cream, with
purple staining at the posterior margin and between
the teeth.

Other common names:
  Partially-rough Venus
Author of the species, form or variety:
  Wood
Date of publication:
  1828
Average size of mature shell:
  4 cm (1½ in)
Locality:
  Western Central America
Habitat depth:
  Extends to about 25 m (83 ft)
Availability:
  Abundant

Other common names:
  Pokerchip Venus
Author of the species, form or variety:
  Röding
Date of publication:
  1798
Average size of mature shell:
  6 cm (2½ in)
Locality:
  India to Eastern Asia
Habitat depth:
  Extends to about 25 m (83 ft)
Availability:
  Abundant

Pitar · Dione

Description

A much desirable and sought-after species in the 17th and 18th centuries, it is still a popular bivalve. The equal valves have strong concentric flat ridges. Curved and strong spines extend from the ridge which runs from the umbones to the lower posterior margin. The shell is off-white, with pale lavender tints.

Other common names:
  Royal Comb Venus
Author of the species, form or variety:
  L.
Date of publication:
  1758
Average size of mature shell:
  5 cm (2 in)
Locality:
  Caribbean
Habitat depth:
  Extends to about 25 m (83 ft)
Availability:
  Uncommon

Lioconcha · Castrensis

Description

This is a most attractive Venus clam. The rounded-to-oval shell has equal and somewhat inflated valves with fine concentric ridges. It is cream in colour, with hazy greyish blue patches, overlaid with vivid dark brown zigzag lines or tent markings. All the shells here are from the central Philippines.

Other common names:
  Chocolate-flamed Venus
Author of the species, form or variety:
  L.
Date of publication:
  1758
Average size of mature shell:
  5 cm (2 in)
Locality:
  Indo-Pacific
Habitat depth:
  Extends to about 25 m (83 ft)
Availability:
  Common

SUPER FAMILY
PHOLADOIDEA

FAMILY
PHOLADIDAE
(Piddocks or Angel Wings)

This is a family of bivalves that have thin but strong elongated shells that gape at both ends and have ribbed surfaces. Apart from the two main valves, there are various accessory plates. Members of this worldwide group are to be found in Arctic, temperate, and tropical seas. They are able to burrow or bore into various substrates, such as coral, rock, soft limestone and mud, as well as man-made materials like wooden harbour piles. Of the several genera, Pholas, Barnea and Cyrtopleura are the best known.

Cyrtopleura · Costata

Description

Unlike the rather drab *P. dactylus*, this species is very beautiful, with elongated and inflated white valves. The sculpturing consists of raised and scaly radial ridges and fine concentric lines. Although the specimen shown exceeds 19 cm (7H in), specimens are rarely larger than 13 cm (5 in). The current size record is 20 cm (8 in).

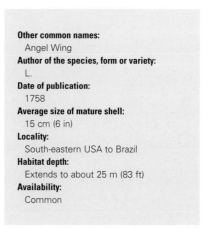

Other common names:
  Angel Wing
Author of the species, form or variety:
  L.
Date of publication:
  1758
Average size of mature shell:
  15 cm (6 in)
Locality:
  South-eastern USA to Brazil
Habitat depth:
  Extends to about 25 m (83 ft)
Availability:
  Common

Class
Polyplacophora

Known as chitons or 'coat of mail' shells and much resembling woodlice, these possess eight segmented plates which are held together by a leathery and tough band known as a 'girdle.' They have either a broad or narrow foot and microsensory organs which are situated on the shell and girdle surfaces. They lack tentacles. There may be 600 or so species.

ORDER
NEOLORICATA

This is a large class of molluscs, known as chitons or coat-of-mail shells. The group contains about 1,000 species of more or less ovate shells, consisting of eight overlapping plates which can, in a limited fashion, move between each other (hence 'coat of mail'). These plates are set into a tough muscular material known as the girdle. The chitons are vegetarian and usually inhabit rocky shallow water. They eat after dusk – usually small algae and, on rare occasions, small invertebrates. The arrangement of this class is complex. There is one order, Neoloricata; then three suborders and nine super families. Of the many genera, we are interested here in only two; other well-known ones are Stenoplax, Mopalia and Tonicella.

Dinoplax · Gigas

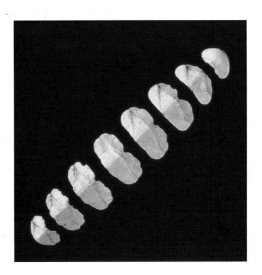

Description

This specimen has had the tough leathery girdle removed to show the eight separate plates that make up chiton shells. The last small plate had a minutely serrated margin which resembles a miniature half-set of dentures! These end plates, which are often found on beaches, are frequently known as 'false teeth' locally.

Other common names:
  Giant South African Chiton
Author of the species, form or variety:
  Gmelin
Date of publication:
  1792
Average size of mature shell:
  10 cm (4 in)
Locality:
  South Africa
Habitat depth:
  Extends to about 25 m (83 ft)
Availability:
  Common

Dinoplax · Gigas

Description

The largest of the South African chitons, it has thick
and solid plates. The specimen shown here has had
the girdle removed and, because of its relative
immaturity, the fine surface sculpturing can be seen.
On large shells, the exterior is usually encrusted. The
underside of the plates is off-white. Shells are often
found washed up on beaches.

Other common names:
   Giant South African Chiton
Author of the species, form or variety:
   Gmelin
Date of publication:
   1792
Average size of mature shell:
   10 cm (4 in)
Locality:
   South Africa
Habitat depth:
   Extends to about 25 m (83 ft)
Availability:
   Common

Chiton · Tulipa

Description

A prettily marked and coloured species, it is narrow
and elongated with a high central ridge. The pattern
and colours can be very variable, although the
underside of the plates is generally a bright bluish
green.

Other common names:
   Tulip Chiton
Author of the species, form or variety:
   Quoy and Gaimard
Date of publication:
   1834
Average size of mature shell:
   4 cm (1½ in)
Locality:
   South Africa
Habitat depth:
   Extends to about 25 m (83 ft)
Availability:
   Common

Class

Cephalopoda

This is a relatively small group of highly mobile molluscs that possess large eyes, tentacles with suckers and powerful beak-like mouths. All species are carnivorous. These creatures are most unlike other molluscs – especially as far as the soft parts are concerned. Some do possess an external shell, such as the Nautilus, while others, such as Spirula, have internal shells. Other species such as the octopus and squids, have no shell at all.

FAMILY
NAUTILIDAE
(Chambered Nautilus Shells)

This is a small family of perhaps four or five species. The arrangement of these shells is in need of revision, due to confusion in specific names and local variants. There is a subclass and an order – Nautiloidea and Nautilida respectively. They have external shells, the animal occupying the last and largest chamber. The shell itself is large and coiled, and closely resembles the Ammonite, its fossil ancestor, of which there were once many. There is one genus, Nautilus.

Nautilus · Pompilius

Description

This well-known species has a large and coiled shell, with an indented (involute) spire and large and gaping aperture (the male tends to have a larger aperture). The shell is off-white, with distinctive tan, 'flame'-like radial bands. There is a black calloused area facing the aperture on the compressed part of the coiled shell. Unlike other species, this has no umbilicus. The half-section clearly shows the internal chambers which are used ingeniously as a buoyancy aid.

Other common names:
  Common Chambered Nautilus
Author of the species, form or variety:
  L.
Date of publication:
  1758
Average size of mature shell:
  15 cm (6 in)
Locality:
  Western Pacific
Habitat depth:
  Between 25 and 500 m (83–1,650 ft)
Availability:
  Common

FAMILY
SPIRULIDAE
(Spirulas)

Closely related to the Nautilus, this family of one species consists of a thin, fragile, closely coiled shell with internal chambers. The animal, a small deep-sea squid, entirely covers its shell when alive. It is within the subclass Coleoidea and order Sepiida. Many hundreds of these shells are regularly discovered washed up on beaches in numerous worldwide warm sea areas. There is one genus, Spirula.

Spirula · Spirula

Description

The species lives in depths of about 1,000 m (3,300 ft) and is usually only beach-collected. Through the thin walls of the coiled off-white shell the partitions inside can be clearly seen. The thin divisional walls are nacreous, and one can be seen at the open end.

Other common names:
  Common Spirula
Author of the species, form or variety:
  L.
Date of publication:
  1758
Average size of mature shell:
  2.5 cm (1 in)
Locality:
  Worldwide in warm seas
Habitat depth:
  Between 150–500 m (495–1,650 ft)
Availability:
  Common

SUPER FAMILY
ARGONAUTOIDEA

FAMILY
ARGONAUTIDAE
(Paper Nautilus)

Argonauts are octopus-like animals which do not have true shells, producing instead a shell-like egg case which in shape is most beautiful. The 'arms' of the female secrete the material to form the shell as a receptacle in which to cradle the tiny eggs. There are less than a dozen known species, all of which inhabit warm open seas. Many such egg cases are found washed ashore after storms, but they are often incomplete. These shells are very popular collectors' items.

Argonauta · Nodosa

Description

While similar in shape to *A. argo*, this has a wider keeled area, its sides are more inflated, and the sculpturing is nodulose and not ridged. The shell is rather more thickened and heavy, but still fragile. Like other species of paper nautilus, they can occur in one locality in great numbers and then vanish for years – obviously seasons and ocean currents are to be taken into consideration when accounting for this phenomenon.

Other common names:
Knobbed Paper Nautilus
Author of the species, form or variety:
Lightfoot
Date of publication:
1786
Average size of mature shell:
18 cm (7 in)
Locality:
Indo-Pacific
Habitat depth:
Extends to about 25 m (83 ft)
Availability:
Common

Argonauta · Argo

Description

This beautiful, delicate structure is very thin and lightweight. There are numerous low wavy radial ridges extending from the narrowly coiled spire to the margin, where a double row of short, sharp nodules extends in a keel-like fashion around the shell. The shell is off-white to cream in colour, the early part of the keel and spines being tinted with greyish black.

Other common names:
  Common Paper Nautilus
Author of the species, form or variety:
  L.
Date of publication:
  1758
Average size of mature shell:
  20 cm (8 in)
Locality:
  Worldwide in warm seas
Habitat depth:
  Extends to about 25 m (83 ft)
Availability:
  Common

Argonauta · Hians

Description

A much smaller, more inflated shell than A. *argo* this has fewer and proportionally larger keel nodules. In some, two prominent and sharp projections form outwardly either side of the aperture margin adjacent to the spire. This can be seen in the darker form, which is from the Gulf of Oman; the large pale shell is from the Philippines.

Other common names:
  Brown Paper Nautilus
Author of the species, form or variety:
  Lightfoot
Date of publication:
  1786
Average size of mature shell:

Locality:
  warm Pacific and Atlantic and Indian Oceans
Habitat depth:
  25 m (83 ft)
Availability:
  Common

Class
Scaphopoda

A small class of 200–400 species, these are known as tusk or tooth shells and are the most primitive of all molluscs. They have a long, narrow, tubular shell which is open at both ends. The narrower posterior end usually protrudes above the sand in which most species live. They have no head, eyes or gills, but possess a large foot and a radula.

FAMILY
DENTALIIDAE
(Tusk Shells)

There are at least 1,000 known species of tusk shells, many of which are very small. They occur in worldwide locations, inhabiting either shallow or, more likely, deep water, where they burrow in sand or mud with their posterior end exposed. Their range extends from temperate to tropical seas. The species vary little and are generally curved, long, tapering at the posterior and hollow. In some shells the posterior portion has a notch or slit, or a small terminal 'pipe.' They are a carnivorous group, feeding on protozoans, foraminifera and other micro-organisms. The family has only luke-warm popularity among collectors.

Dentalium · Formosum

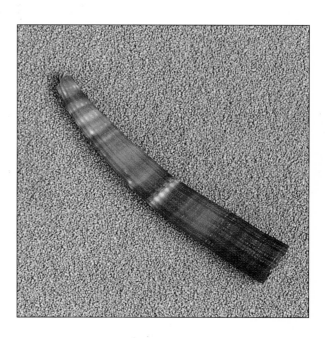

Description

A relatively short and stocky species, it has numerous low longitudinal ribs. At the narrowed posterior, there is a short open terminal pipe. The shell is most attractive in colour, graduating from maroon to a dull brick red with odd spiral bands of cream or white. The species inhabits fairly shallow water, but is only infrequently offered, usually from Japanese waters.

Dentalium Octangulatum (Octagonal Tusk)

Other common names:
 Formosan Tusk
Author of the species, form or variety:
 Adams and Reeve
Date of publication:
 1850
Average size of mature shell:
 7.5 cm (3 in)
Locality:
 Japan to the Philippines
Habitat depth:
 Extends to about 25 m (83 ft)
Availability:
 Uncommon

Glossary

axial – following or parallel to the shell axis, usually applied to gastropods.

axis – an imaginary line around which the whorls revolve, drawn from the anterior to the apex of gastropods.

beads – very small, usually rounded knobs, these are often spirally laid, resembling a string of beads.

body whorl – the largest section of a gastropod, this encloses the soft parts.

byssal/byssus – some bivalves have a byssal area, through which the byssus (fine, thread-like filaments) extend for anchorage.

calcareous – a chalky, usually white appearance, due primarily to the presence of calcium carbonate.

callous – a thickened, often smooth area, usually found around the aperture or on the parietal wall.

cancellation – a sculptured area of lines crossing others at right angles, in a lattice-like effect; also referred to as reticulation.

carina – a sharp ridge or keel.

columella – the spirally-twisting pillar surrounding the axis of a gastropod.

concentric – following the direction of growth lines, usually in bivalves.

cord – rope-like ornamentation, usually spiral.

coronated – having nodules on the shoulder or spine; crown-like.

corrugated – structured with ridges or folds.

crenulation – notches or small indentations on ridges or margins.

dead-collected – a shell devoid of its animal; often found on beaches, such shells are sometimes referred to as 'beached.'

denticle – a small tooth-like projection; shells with denticles around the margins or inside the lip are 'dentate' or 'denticulate.'

dorsum – the back of a shell, opposite the aperture.

endemic – confined to a restricted area or geographical region.

fasciole – a groove or raised spiral band, formed by successive growth stages and found at the base of certain gastropods.

fimbriate – edged or bordered by thin, wavy sculpturing or an ornamental nature.

frondose – leaf-like.

funicular – a pad-like calloused area found on or above the umbilical portion of some moon snails.

fusiform – spindle-shaped.

globose – rounded or almost spherical.

impressed – indented – a term usually applied to the suture.

keel – a raised, often sharp ridge or carina.

lamellate – covered with thin scales or plates.

lirae – fine ridges, often found on the inner surface of the outer lip.

lunule – **a** small or narrow crescent – a special area in front of the beak of many bivalve shells.

maculated – irregularly blotched or spotted.

nacreous – resembling mother-of-pearl.

nodule – a sharp or rounded knob or node; where several are present, the shell is described as nodulose.

ocellated – having eye-like spots.

operculum – grown on the foot of many species of gastropod, this is an oval or rounded structure that seals the aperture when the animal withdraws into its shell.

ovate – oval.

pallial line – a curved scar line seen on the interior walls of bivalve shells at the point where the edges of the mantle were attached.

parietal area/wall – occasionally referred to as the inner lip, this is the area in gastropods that lies opposite the outer lip and above the columella.

periostracum – the fibrous and skin-like outer covering of many shells.

plicate – braided or folded portions of the columella; bearing plicate.

porcellaneous – a porcelain or china-like texture.

process – a spine or projection.

protoconch – the tip or apex of a gastropod, formed in its larval stage.

pustulose – a surface covered with pustules or tiny pimple-like swellings.

pyriform – pear-shaped.

radial – ray-like ornamentation or sculpturing, diverging from the umbones of bivalves.

reticulation – a pattern of oblique intersecting ridges or striae; also known as cancellation.

rib – a raised or elevated structure, usually laid parallel to the axis.

scabrous – a rough, scaly surface.

stria/striae – fine raised or grooved line(s) on the surface of a shell, sometimes an indication of growth stages.

suture – the junction of two whorls, it is often depressed or indented.

threads – very fine sculptural lines, usually in a spiral pattern.

trigonal – triangular.

trochoidal – shaped like a spinning top; rounded at the bottom and tapering to the top, as in top shells.

truncated – finished off abruptly; a term often applied to bivalves with a square-ended appearance and to gastropods with abruptly-terminated spires.

tubercule – a projection, usually rounded, that is larger than a pustule but smaller than a nodule.

umbilicus – the lower open axis around which the whorls of a gastropod are coiled.

umbo – sometimes referred to as the beak, this is the part of a bivalve that is the first to be formed; the plural is umbones.

varix – a growth resting stage that often appears as a raised and thickened ridge; murex shells bear several varices.

veliger – a mollusc in its young, free-swimming larval stage.

ventral – in gastropods, the surface on the same side as the aperture; in bivalves, the portion opposite the hinge, where the valves are widest.

whorl – a complete coil of a gastropod shell.

Index to common names

Index to Latin names